Issues in Focus

The Crime of Genocide

Terror Against Humanity

Ray Spangenburg and Kit Moser

Enslow Publishers, Inc.

40 Industrial Road   PO Box 38
Box 398   Aldershot
Berkeley Heights, NJ 07922   Hants GU12 6BP
USA   UK

http://www.enslow.com

In Memory of Robert C. Norton

Library of Congress Cataloging-in-Publication Data

Spangenburg, Ray, 1939–
    The crime of genocide : terror against humanity / Ray
Spangenburg and Kit Moser.
        p. cm. – (Issues in focus)
    Summary: Examines the horror of genocide throughout history,
with a focus on the 20th century. The Holocaust as well as genocide
in Rwanda, Kosovo, Bosnia, and Cambodia are all discussed. Ways
to prevent genocide from ever happening again are also explored.
    ISBN 0-7660-1249-2 (hard : alk. paper)
    1. Genocide. 2. Crimes against humanity—History—20th century.
3. Genocide—History—20th century. I. Moser, Kit, 1944–
II. Title. III. Issues in focus (Hillside, N.J.).
HV6322.7 .S65 2000
364.15'1—dc21   99-050818
                                                         CIP

Printed in the United States of America

10 9 8 7 6 5 4 3 2

To Our Readers: We have done our best to make sure all Internet addresses in this book were active and appropriate when we went to press. However, the author and the publisher have no control over and assume no liability for the material available on those Internet sites or on other Web sites they may link to. Any comments or suggestions can be sent by e-mail to comments@enslow.com or to the address on the back cover.

Illustration Credits: Central State Archive of Film, Photo, and Photographic Documents, Courtesy of USHMM Photo Archives, p. 25; Corbis/Bettmann, Photo by David Schwab, p. 57; Courtesy of Deutches Literaturarchiv, Marbach and Armenian National Institute, Photo by Armin T. Wegner, pp. 47, 53; Jim Mendenhall, © 1993, Courtesy Simon Wiesenthal Center Museum of Tolerance, p. 110; National Archives, pp. 12, 34, 42, 90; UNHCR/R, H. J. Davies, p. 74; UNHCR/R, R. Chalasani, p. 86; UNHCR/R, A. Hollman, p. 81; UNHCR/R. LeMoyne, pp. 13, 79, 85; UNHCR/R, P. Moumtzis, p. 69; UNHCR/R, B. Press, p. 72; UN Photo/J. Issac, pp. 60, 63.

Cover Illustration: Central State Archive of Film, Photo, and Photographic Documents, Courtesy of Photo Archives.

Cover Description: These children were found alive in a concentration camp after Germany surrendered at the end of World War II.

Contents

Acknowledgments 4

Prologue 5

1 Genocide: The Slaying
of a People 7

2 The Holocaust:
Massacre of Millions 19

3 The Holocaust: Why? 38

4 Armenian Genocide: The
Denial of Mass Murder 45

5 Cambodia: A People
Turned on Itself 54

6 Rwanda: Incited Massacre 65

7 Bosnia and Kosovo: Genocide
and "Ethnic Cleansing" 76

8 Genocide and the
Scales of Justice 88

9 What Can We Do? 101

Chapter Notes 112

Glossary 119

Further Reading 121

Organizations to Contact 122

Internet Addresses 124

Places to Visit 125

Index 126

Acknowledgments

Several individuals went to special effort to help with our research, including: Chris Sims of the USHMM Photo Archives; Dr. Rouben Adalian, director of the Armenian National Institute; Sybil Stevens; Anneliese Hollmann and Anne Kellner of the Office of the UN High Commissioner for Refugees; Joyce Rosenblum of the United Nations Photo Unit; and Marcial Laviña of the Simon Wiesenthal Center.

Prologue

The notices were posted on walls and fences ten days after the German army captured the city of Kiev in the Ukraine. All Jews in the area were ordered to report with all of their belongings for "resettlement."

The notices lied.

Now the soldiers with the guns waited while the Jews moved in long lines toward them. The ravine was long and deep in this place called Babi Yar, near the Ukrainian city of Kiev. The Jews in the front of the lines were naked. Farther down the lines others were being forced to take off their clothes and throw them into the ever-growing piles of discarded garments and belongings alongside the road. Men, women, and children marched naked. Some were silent, some crying. Some struggled, only to be forced back into the lines by soldiers, policemen, and dogs. In the end, they all took their places along the edge of the high precipice. Behind them others waited their turn. The lines stretched far back, toward the city. From where they waited on the opposite side of the ravine the soldiers could not see the end of the lines.

Below the soldiers' feet, inside the ravine itself, were thousands of the dead and dying. Silent corpses, their arms and legs already stiffening, were piled alongside the not yet dead. No one heeded their last movements and anguished cries. Occasionally a soldier would aim his rifle and fire down into the ravine at one of the naked bodies that was still moving. It was something to do while dozens more Jews were herded into position along the edges of the ravine across from them. Some of the soldiers smoked cigarettes and joked. Then, receiving their signal, the soldiers would raise the rifles and machine guns and fire. With each volley, more Jews fell into the pit. The bodies of the naked men, women, and children crowded the pit, as the piles grew higher throughout the day.

For two days it continued.

By the end of those two days in September 1941, more than thirty-five thousand bodies lay piled in grotesque, nightmarish heaps in the ravine.

By the end of the year, more than one hundred thousand Jews would be murdered at Babi Yar, their bodies tossed or fallen into the pit.

Babi Yar was not the only killing place.

Between the years 1941 and 1945, under cover of World War II, over 6 million Jews were murdered under the leadership of Adolf Hitler and the Nazi party. It was the worst genocide in human history.

But there have been many other genocides.

They happened because people hated, were afraid, and wanted another entire group or race of people to die and vanish forever from the face of the earth.

1

Genocide:
The Slaying
of a People

"The twentieth century is the most violent and murderous in history."

—Eric Markusen, sociologist[1]

The word "genocide" means, literally, "the killing of a people."

Every culture recognizes that killing people is immoral. No one denies that murdering an entire group of people—numbering in the hundreds, thousands, or millions—is one of the most horrible crimes humans have ever committed.

Yet, somehow, people find ways of justifying mass murder. Bystanders have watched without protest. Soldiers, police, militia, and neighbors have systematically ended the existence of entire tribes or groups of people and cultures. Sometimes, someone makes an objection, but then nothing happens. No consequences befall those who committed the crime. Examples in history of this pattern occur again and again. A look at any city's daily newspaper or any online newspaper reveals that the pattern continues to haunt us today.

The word "genocide"—referring to the systematic killing of an entire group, or people—is relatively new. The practice of genocide, however, is not.

Genocide's Past

Genocide has a long history. Conquerors have committed genocide for thousands of years. Often, they have even been cheered and celebrated as heroes.

Attila swooped through Europe with his warriors in the fifth century and brutally attacked countless numbers of innocent people. In the thirteenth century the Mongol warrior Genghis Khan conquered most of the regions between the Yellow Sea (off the east coast of China) and the Black Sea (north of Turkey). His military forces are said to have committed terrible atrocities against many of the peoples they conquered, including unknown numbers of Chinese, Muslims, and Persians. Yet he is known primarily as a great military leader and the creator of a stable political system.

Genocide has often been committed in the name

of "cleansing" or "purifying." Those who murder say they are trying to get rid of a group of people they think are undesirable. Or they want to wipe out ideas or religious beliefs they consider evil. In thirteenth-century Europe, representatives of the Christian church based in Rome committed genocide when a religious group called the Albigenses or Cathari questioned church doctrine and threatened the dominance of the Roman church.

Between 1881 and 1921, mobs in Ukraine and throughout eastern Europe waged pogroms—destructive and murderous mob attacks—against Jews living in those regions. Thousands were killed. The tsarist government made no move to stop the carnage, and even encouraged the killing through its anti-Semitic policies. The years of revolution in Russia, from 1917 to 1921, brought even worse pogroms against the Jews—partly because they were attacked by people on all sides of the conflict. During these four years, more than sixty thousand Jews were exterminated in Russia.

Forced Famine in Ukraine

The Russian Revolution of 1917 and the following civil wars ended the three-hundred-year reign of the tsarist Romanovs. A new communist government replaced the old regime. Communism embraces the idea that all property should belong to the entire community, not individuals, and that it should be distributed by the state according to need. However, the new government and its policies in Russia brought new terrors. By 1929, Joseph Stalin had taken complete control and imposed his brutal policies on the entire Union of Soviet Socialist Republics (USSR), which included Russia and Ukraine. He sought to build the economy through a series of steps that required extreme sacrifice, especially on the part of peasant farmers. Over the objection of the kulaks, the prosperous farmers of Ukraine, he abolished private possession of farmland. Because of their independence and opposition to his policies, Stalin believed these farmers to be "enemies of the people."

Stalin called for liquidation of the kulak as a class. He set state-required production quotas so high that even the most productive farm could not possibly raise enough crops to meet them. The government seized all the food the kulaks raised—every grain of wheat and every vegetable. The kulaks were doomed to starve.

Later even the Soviet government criticized this and others of Stalin's cruel policies. In 1964, a Soviet writer named Mikhael Alekseev gave this account of the famine: "In accordance with one order or another, all the grain and all the fodder were taken away. Horses began to die en masse and in 1933 there was a terrible famine. Whole families died, houses fell apart, village streets grew empty. . . ."[2]

During the years 1931–1933, as many as 6 million to 10 million people died of starvation in Ukraine—by a famine induced artificially and purposefully by their government.[3]

Killing for Land in America

Many native peoples have suffered genocide at the hands of settlers who have seized, or colonized, their lands. No one knows how many American Indians in the New World died at the hands of Spanish, Portuguese, British, and French explorers during the 1400 to 1600s, but certainly the numbers are in the millions.[4]

Later, when European colonists arrived in New England, they almost completely wiped out the Pequot tribe that lived there. Between 1630 and 1638 New England Puritans and their Indian allies massacred between fifty thousand and one hundred thousand Pequot. At the height of the campaign, on May 26, 1637, a band of white soldiers joined forces with American Indian enemies of the Pequot to burn their main village and slaughter its residents. Today, the Pequot are nearly extinct—only 539 remained at the time of the 1990 census.

During much of the nineteenth century, the U.S. Army and the American Indian Plains dwellers of the West fought in many sporadic battles. Among the most deadly confrontations was the tragic massacre at Wounded Knee, South Dakota, in 1890. As about two hundred fifty Lakota prepared to surrender, they were shot down by nearly five hundred heavily armed U.S. Cavalry troops. The frozen ground was strewn with the bodies of the victims, cut down as they fled on foot across the open plain, where there was no cover or place of safety. This tragic slaughter did not eradicate the Lakota, or their Ghost Dance

A Lakota campsite in 1891, near the site of the tragic massacre at Wounded Knee.

rituals, which many Lakota practiced to give them power over the settlers and the military. However, Wounded Knee came to symbolize the U.S. government's efforts to put an end to Indian possession of the vast Plains territory and to control their culture—efforts that might be called ethnocide, the systematic destruction of a people by destroying its culture. It is part of the arsenal of genocide.

Twentieth-Century Genocide Explosion

Genocide is not new, but it recently has become much worse. Despite these historic examples and many others, nothing equaled the scale of the bloodbaths of the twentieth century. In the last half of the century alone genocides occurred in Indonesia (1965–1966), East Timor (1975–1979), Bangladesh (1971), Burundi (1972), Cambodia (1975–1979), Rwanda (1994), Bosnia-Herzegovina (1990s), and Kosovo (1999).[5] Genocide also occurred in Nanking, Tibet, Burma, Argentina, and El Salvador. Six major genocides, claiming more than one to two million lives each, occurred between the years 1900 and 2000. Among those, we explore five, including the recent atrocities inflicted by ethnic groups in the

Refugees driven from their homes in Kosovo arrive in Albania, June 1998.

former Yugoslavia and Rwanda, for the lessons they teach us.

One expert estimates that as many as 60 million[6] and another asserts more than 119 million[7] people died in genocides between 1900 and 1995. Completely accurate figures are hard to come by, but that is nearly one-quarter to one-half of the 1990 population of the United States.

Genocide Defined

In 1944, Raphael Lemkin, a well-regarded expert in international law, came up with the word "genocide" by blending the Greek word *genos* (a people or tribe) and the Latin suffix *-cidium* (killing). He had seen the need for a word to describe a particular type of crime against humanity: the systematic, intentional murder of an entire people.

The reason Lemkin and others saw that need is described in part in the prologue of this book. During the years 1939 to 1945, German Nazis—and others who helped them—tortured, mutilated, and killed more than 6 million Jews. This Holocaust was an attempt by Nazi Germany to liquidate (completely destroy) all Jews—men, women, and children. In his native Poland, Lemkin's own family was wiped out. The Nazis also tried to exterminate other groups they considered undesirable, including homosexuals, Roma (Gypsies), the disabled, and the mentally ill. Altogether, the Nazis killed about 11 million people.

By 1948, genocide had become such an urgent international problem that it was among the earliest problems considered by the United Nations (UN), an international body formed in 1945 to promote peace. The UN General Assembly adopted the Convention on the Prevention and Punishment of the Crime of Genocide on December 9, 1948, which included the worldwide standard definition. It states:

> In the present Convention, genocide means any of the following acts committed with intent to destroy, in whole or in part, a national, ethnical, racial or religious group, as such:
>
> (a) Killing members of the group;
>
> (b) Causing serious bodily or mental harm to members of the group;
>
> (c) Deliberately inflicting on the group conditions of life calculated to bring about its physical destruction in whole or in part;
>
> (d) Imposing measures intended to prevent births within the group;
>
> (e) Forcibly transferring children of the group to another group.[8]

Why Remember?

As one Holocaust survivor said tiredly, "What do I think about remembering? I say, it is past. Let it go. It's over."[9]

No memorial will bring back those who were mercilessly killed. It may not even serve to ease the pain of the living. Yet many people believe that the past should not be ignored. Many also believe that people have a responsibility to watch and act on signs of genocide. Learning about past destruction is a way to learn how to recognize and act to stop genocide from now on.

Examples of Genocide

In this book, we focus on five examples of twentieth-century genocide. Only three of them fit the United Nations definition: the Holocaust, the Armenian genocide, and massacres that took place in Rwanda in 1994. In addition to those, we discuss two other major cases of mass murder that many experts consider also to be cases of genocide: the killing fields of Cambodia and the more varied forms of ethnic cleansing, ethnocide, and mass murder in the former Yugoslavia.

What happened in Cambodia is technically outside the United Nations definition. The Cambodian government executed more than one million of its own people. They were not different from other groups ethnically or culturally. They practiced no different religion. They were not physically different. Instead, the government believed these people disagreed with official policy and held differing political views, a matter not covered in the United Nations definition. However, many critics of the usual definition of genocide believe that mass murder for political views should be included.

The Prosecutor for the International Criminal Tribunal for the former Yugoslavia (ICTY) has handed down indictments against leaders in the

Balkan countries for genocide, among other crimes. For technical reasons, many analysts do not see the Balkan struggle as primarily genocidal, but in fact, official sanction and direct orders have been given many times for mass murder in these countries since Slovenia and Croatia declared independence from Yugoslavia in 1991.

Responsibility for Genocide

The crime of genocide imposes many difficult challenges. The international community has recognized the need to decide who is responsible for a genocide, but making that judgment is very difficult. The leaders of a country often have the power either to provoke or stop the crime. Soldiers, paratroopers, and citizens carry out orders, and bystanders are often forced to participate in the slaughter, or they may do nothing to prevent it. Those who do attempt prevention may become victims themselves. Leaders of other countries may stand by without intervening, and the people in those countries may remain unconcerned, oblivious, or even uninformed. Judging responsibility is extremely complex, but it is crucial if genocide is to be stopped. There must also be consequences, but until the last fifty years, most perpetrators of genocide have faced few consequences, or none at all. That has only just begun to change.

Finally, we must find ways to prevent genocide and mass killing—from the international to the national and local government level, and down to the personal level of every individual in every country of the world. Surrounded as we are by continuing violence and aggression, people must work especially hard to find ways to resolve differences constructively.

These questions and challenges have no easy answers. They are among the biggest that face human civilization in the twenty-first century.

2

The Holocaust: Massacre of Millions

"Never again!"

—Jewish promise after the Holocaust

The Holocaust took place in Nazi Germany close to mid-century, between the years 1939 and 1945. The people behind this atrocity killed two-thirds of all Jews living in Europe during World War II. It is a unique case, and yet at the same time it has connections with all the other genocides that have occurred in the last century.

The German government under Hitler had committed itself to what became known as the Final Solution to the "Jewish

19

problem." The expression was a cover-up for the planned, systematic extermination of European Jews.

Anti-Semitism: Scourge of the Centuries

Wherever Jews live, they often are proud to preserve their own heritage and culture, just as Italian Americans, Filipino Americans, Irish Americans, Chinese Americans, African Americans, or American Indians do in the United States.

People are frequently fearful and suspicious of what they think is the Other. What is not understood is often hated, and people, especially in groups, readily prey on any group that seems obviously different. Throughout the ages, Jews have suffered repeated discrimination—so often, in fact, that being anti-Jewish has a name of its own: anti-Semitism.

People have traveled down the path of anti-Semitism many times, and never justly. The Roman Empire rarely gave citizenship to Jews. In medieval times, the Catholic Church persecuted Jews, especially during the Inquisition. Because church and state were often one government, any non-Christian had a hard time during these centuries, and the Jews consistently were subject to restrictions, second-class citizenship, and outright attacks.

In many parts of Europe, Jews were forced to live in special sections of cities, in Italy first called ghettos. (Ghetto was a Venetian word referring to the foundry located on the island where Jews were forced to live in the 1600s.) Ghettos were usually walled, and all residents had to be inside the walls before curfew. Part of the reason for this arrangement was economic—non-Jewish shopkeepers and businessmen wanted to keep their Jewish competitors under control. Many Jews settled in Eastern Europe from about 1096 on and again after the Black Death (also called the plague, 1348), when people in other parts of Europe blamed them for its spread, claiming that they had poisoned the well water and caused the disease. Some people believed that Jews were agents of the devil. Others blamed Jews for the death of Jesus. (After many centuries, the Second Vatican Council, a governing body of the Roman Catholic Church, formally condemned this charge in 1965.)

After the Middle Ages, in Eastern Europe and Russia especially, Jews became the targets of rigorous restrictions. Russia passed laws that prevented Jews from owning land and restricted the number who could attend colleges or universities. In 1792, Russia designated a large area in its western regions as the Pale of Settlement, where the Jewish population was required to live. A series of pogroms broke out in 1881 in Russia, and recurred in the years that followed between 1881 and 1917. The worst pogroms occurred during the civil war that broke out in Russia from 1917 to 1921, when more than sixty thousand Jews were killed.

In Germany, anti-Semitism had become extreme by the nineteenth century. Germans referred to their discomfort about Jews in German society as the "Jewish problem." Philosophers and theologians became obsessed by the topic. At least twelve hundred publications in Germany between 1870 and

1900, most of them anti-Semitic, were devoted to the "Jewish problem."[1] Anti-Semitism had crept into all aspects of German culture, and had become a topic of constant debate and discussion. Even children's books portrayed Jews as monstrous. Many Germans began to see Jews not only as evil, or as agents of the devil, but virtually as the devil himself. People began to talk and write seriously about the need to stamp out this evil, to exterminate the Jews.

At the end of the nineteenth century, German philosophers also became interested in the concept of race as a way of making divisions among humans. As many seemingly scientific facts were gathered and much discussion and analysis took place, Germans had a new way of separating themselves from Jews. They saw Jews as a different race.

Anti-Jewish feeling grew worse after the end of World War I, when the German economy was in trouble, and many people were short of food and money. People easily believed that their troubles were caused by the Jews. The Jews became the scapegoat for everyone else's woes, or, as described by political science scholar Daniel Jonah Goldhagen, they became seen as "the source of, and . . . more or less identified with, everything awry with the world."[2] People referred to Jews as parasites who lived off society, having no country of their own. They perceived Jews as lazy and unwilling to work and referred to them as "riffraff."

Yet the Jews had committed no more crimes than anyone else did. Their crime was that they were different. And for this they were subjected to intense suspicion, hatred, and even fear.

Background: The Rise of the "Master Race"

World War I (1914–1918) had been one of the bloodiest wars ever, and when it was over, the Allies (Great Britain, France, Russia, and others, including the United States) were bitter, even though they had won. Germany, the main aggressor, had caused many deaths and much destruction, so the Allies demanded that they pay for the damages caused by the war, and they required high reparation payments (compensation for damages) as part of the peace treaty.

Germany, though, had overextended its economy while waging war and had suffered damages and losses as well. The German people were depressed both psychologically and economically. The economy improved briefly, but then plunged again when the worldwide Depression began in 1930.

That was when an intense young man named Adolf Hitler and his political party, the National Socialist German Workers, began to attract a lot of attention. The Nazis, as Hitler's political party was called, talked about the superiority of Germany. Hitler said the Aryan race of white, blond, blue-eyed, German-speaking peoples was superior. He encouraged Germans to be proud of their heritage. They were the "master race," which would rightfully inherit the earth. He made the Germans feel strong again.

In 1933, President von Hindenburg of Germany

appointed Hitler chancellor, hoping to please the people who liked what they heard from the Nazis. He thought he could control the short man with a little mustache and a way with rhetoric. But he was wrong. Soon Hitler had abolished civil liberties in Germany and became a dictator.

The Warning Signs

Hitler began to put the pressure on German Jews even before he became chancellor, and he increased the pressure between 1933 and 1938. The Nazis boycotted Jewish businesses and restricted Jewish entry into professions and schools with a quota system. Then, in 1935, the Nuremberg Laws were passed. These laws defined who was a Jew—not by religious practices or beliefs, but by bloodlines. Conversion to Christianity did not matter, so many people who did not embrace Judaism or Jewish heritage or religion were still defined as Jews. The Nuremberg Laws officially stripped all Jews of their citizenship. Jews could not be civil servants. Intermarriage between Jews and Gentiles (non-Jews) was forbidden.

Both officials and citizens joined in to make Jewish lives miserable. Towns posted signs declaring "Jews Not Wanted Here," or "Jews Enter Here at Their Own Risk." Individuals and groups attacked Jewish businesses, cemeteries, and synagogues. In some towns, people who visited Jewish businesses were photographed, and the photographs were posted in public. Jewish businesses were identified

These Jewish children were found alive at the Auschwitz II (Birkenau) concentration camp by liberators when Germany surrendered. This picture was posed after liberation.

and became sites for demonstrations. Jews were routinely attacked, beaten, yelled at, and humiliated.

While the first concentration camps were built at Dachau, Buchenwald, and Oranienburg as early as 1933, at first they were used primarily for political prisoners; of the one thousand Germans imprisoned in Dachau in April 1933, only one hundred were Jews. But the groundwork was laid for terrors to come. By 1937, the number of Jews at Dachau had risen to three hundred, and by 1942, imprisonment in a concentration camp meant nearly certain death to Jews, although the death rate among other prisoners was below 2 percent in 1943.[3] During Hitler's rule, the Nazis built more than ten thousand camps designed to detain prisoners without warrant or trial—concentration camps like Dachau; work camps, where slave labor was used; extermination camps designed to kill; and dozens of other types.

Setting the Stage

Hitler had also established two main police forces: (1) The SS (Schutzstaffel, or "defense echelon"), a special security force founded in 1925 as Hitler's personal bodyguard. (2) The Gestapo (Geheime Staatspolizei, or secret state police), founded in 1933. In 1936, Hitler made the Gestapo a national police force and outlawed judicial appeals against its decisions.

To most people within Germany, things seemed to be going very well by the mid-1930s. The Nazi party had lowered unemployment by hiring people to work on public works projects. Renewed business confidence and rearmament had improved the economy. Hitler appointed Joseph Goebbels head of propaganda, and he did a masterful job of controlling all the media—radio, film, literature, newspapers, theater, and art. He not only squelched criticism, but also painted a euphoric picture of German life.

Meanwhile, most of the world looked the other

way. Most of Europe and the United States were coping with an economic depression as well.

The Night the Synagogues Burned

In November 1938, a minor German embassy official was assassinated in Paris by a Jew who was angered by Nazi treatment of his father. Hitler, of course, blamed all Jews. Under orders, storm troopers streamed into the streets throughout Germany on the nights of November 8 and 9. Jewish shop windows were shattered, and 267 Jewish synagogues were burned. Fire brigades were ordered to protect the surrounding houses, but not to stop the synagogue fires. About twenty thousand people were arrested. Afterward, Jews were charged a $400 million fine for damage done to their own property. That rampage became known as Kristallnacht, the "night of broken glass." It was the beginning of much worse things to come.

The Brink of War

Nazism was the political embodiment of the nationalist fervor promoted by Goebbels with his propaganda machine, advocating totalitarian government, territorial expansion, anti-Semitism, and Aryan supremacy. Now Hitler began to call for the unification of all German-speaking people. He declared that Germany should annex Austria, where German was the national language, and also part of Czechoslovakia, where a large minority of the population in the frontier region was German-speaking.

The Allied leaders of Britain and France, who had formerly placed so many restrictions on Germany, formally agreed to the plan at the Munich Convention of 1938. Jews in all the countries that the Germans occupied also lost their civil rights.

Then on September 1, 1939, Hitler's armies invaded Poland and World War II began as Britain and France reacted. Persecution of the Jews immediately intensified.

The Einsatzgruppen

By late spring of 1941, Hitler was preparing to invade Russia. Once it was conquered and under German power, Hitler planned to make this area a Garden of Eden. He envisioned an area free of all enemies of the German people, and declared his approval of "shooting anyone who even looks askance at us."[4] He referred to anyone who even mildly questioned the actions of the Nazis.

The Nazi government quickly moved to extend this plan to legalize mass murder, a process that had already begun in 1939 in Poland. Orders were given to soldiers to deny prisoner-of-war status to anyone even suspected of anti-German sentiment. These people were to be killed immediately.

A second order was known as the Barbarossa decree. The order gave the German military the right to exterminate any Russian citizen without fear of being tried in a military court. This second edict quickly became interpreted as a directive to destroy all Bolsheviks (Russian communists) and Jews, and the battalions received direct orders to destroy all Jews in the region.

Marked Targets

Beginning on September 1, 1941, all Jews were required to wear a large yellow six-pointed Star of David, marked with the word "Jude" (Jew) in clear black letters. The social isolation of the Jews was now complete. In the 1930s, Germans sometimes bought from Jews or mingled with them socially. Jews had looked the same as other Germans. But with the wearing of the star, everyone now knew who was a Jew.

In late spring, four special units of the SS had been formed. These became the core of the deadly Einsatzgruppen—special execution squads. Some members came from the Gestapo and the Waffen-SS (the military branch of the SS), some from the Order Police (civilian police units). In July, in response to Hitler's directives, Heinrich Himmler (head of both the SS and the Gestapo) increased the Einsatzgruppen by about 16,500 more men, to a total of nearly 20,000.

These mobile units were intended to travel deep into Russia behind the advancing German army. Their job was to clean up or "pacify" the region by exterminating all potential opposition. Their specific purpose was to exterminate the "unwanted," and Jews were first on their list.

These groups cold-bloodedly murdered 1.5 million people. The Jews at Babi Yar represented a small fraction of those who felt the deadly sting of their bullets. Justice Michael Musmanno of the United States, who presided at the Nuremburg trial of the Einsatzgruppen after the war, wrote in his statement that the idea of one million corpses is almost impossible to imagine. Describing the power of the sheer volume of evidence—the careful logs and records kept by the officers themselves—that show the steady growth of the cruel deeds they committed, he wrote:

> However, if one reads through the reports of the Einsatzgruppen and observes the small numbers getting larger, climbing into ten thousand, tens of thousands, a hundred thousand and beyond, then one can at last believe that this actually happened—the cold-blooded, premeditated killing of one million human beings.[5]

Justice Musmanno wrote also about his disbelief that any of that could be possible. He said he would find it easier to imagine water running uphill or trees with roots pointed skyward than to take "at face value these narratives which go beyond the frontiers of human cruelty and savagery." But since the evidence presented came from the reports and statements of the defendants themselves, he concluded, one can "be assured that all this actually happened."[6]

Untrained Killers

In addition to the Einsatzgruppen, who followed the advancing army, other forces were brought into areas closer to Germany. By 1942, after the invasion of Poland, groups of Order Police were brought into

Poland from Germany. The men in the Order Police were generally considered too old for the German army and were drafted instead into these reserve battalions. These men had jobs and families at home. They were not career military soldiers, and most of them had little or no experience with fighting and killing. In his book, *Ordinary Men: Reserve Police Battalion 101 and the Final Solution in Poland*, Christopher R. Browning told the unforgettable story of one such group, Battalion 101. When they were taken early one morning to a sleepy Polish village called Józefów to receive their assignment, their commander, Major Wilhelm Trapp, was hesitant and very upset as he stood before them.

"Pale and nervous, with choking voice and tears in his eyes, Trapp visibly fought to control himself as he spoke," Browning wrote after later interviews with the men.[7] He reminded the men that the Jews had brought on a boycott by the Americans, which had hurt Germany. He told them that some Jews in this village were partisans, subversives who had resisted German occupation of Poland. The Allies, he said, were bombing and killing German women and children. With these rationalizations, he tried to give reason to an unreasonable task, one that he admitted he disliked. Under orders "from the highest authorities," his men were to round up all the Jews in the village. After the men who would be sent to a work camp were separated, all the rest were to be shot—the women, the children, and the elderly.

Then, at the end of his description of their orders, Trapp gave his men an out—an extraordinary gesture in most military settings. If any older men felt unable to go through with the job, he told them, they could step out of the ranks.

Only a handful, about twelve out of almost five hundred, stepped forward. Why? Browning thought many were taken by surprise and did not think to act that quickly. However, conformity and peer pressure also played a big part. When asked later why he had not declined, one mentioned the danger of losing face, and others expressed fear that their buddies would think they were cowards.[8] Many felt the pressure was so great that they had no choice—they did not remember that they ever had another option.

Except for those who dropped out, either at the beginning or after firing a few shots, these men killed or rounded up some fifteen hundred Jews that morning—people they did not know, who had no military connection, and who posed no threat. They did it because they were told to do it.

Later, supposedly out of concern for the psychological well-being of these men and the men of the Einsatzgruppen, Nazi authorities devised more efficient means of achieving their deadly Final Solution.

Death Camps

The best German engineers went to work on the problem, and devised a gas chamber that was effective and fast. They found that large groups of people could be crammed into an airtight building. Then an attendant wearing a gas mask could insert a pellet of poisonous gas in a specially designed grate, which could then be closed from the outside after another attendant closed and locked the door behind the prisoners. Within minutes, the inmates would be dead.

Typically, the extermination site was located out of sight of a camp's prisoners. Prisoners would be herded to the site, told to strip and, especially, remove any jewelry or watches. Women's hair was cut off and saved in warehouses. Then, the prisoners would be told they were entering a shower area. Once inside, they would realize that they were about to die and would begin screaming.

Later, when the people had been killed, the bodies would be removed and cremated in huge ovens for that purpose, or trucked to mass gravesites. These were the last steps in a dehumanizing process that began with arrest and imprisonment.

Arrival

Prisoners were usually arrested without warning and rounded up, then crowded into railway boxcars. They could only guess at their destination. Once they arrived, they would be unloaded onto a shipping dock.

Luciana Nissim, a survivor of Auschwitz, wrote in her diary, "Those who are tired can board the lorries [trucks]—the old, the sick, the children."[9] At the time, this seemed to her like a kind offer. Nissim turned down the offer, though. After the long railway trip standing in a cattle car, she preferred to walk. Her friend, though injured during the journey,

U.S. troops found charred bodies in these furnaces at the Buchenwald concentration camp.

thought they should stick together. So she also walked. Later, to their horror, they discovered that the children, the elderly, and the tired women who chose to travel on the trucks were taken straight to the gas chambers. The Third Reich (as Hitler's regime was called) had no use for those who could not work.

Many of those who were not immediately killed in the concentration camps were worked to death by German factory owners, who used them as slaves. Disease, malnutrition, and starvation were common, and thousands met their deaths in these ways.

According to estimates, between 1.5 million and 4 million people were systematically and efficiently murdered at the extermination camp at Auschwitz alone. This one carefully engineered death machine took the lives of at least one-third of the 5 million to 6 million Jews murdered by the Nazis. Only 7,600 survivors were found there in January 1945, when the advancing Red Army (the army of the USSR) liberated the camp. They were starving, but they were alive—next on the list of executions, but saved. Just before the Soviet soldiers arrived, the Nazis had hurriedly sent more than 58,000 prisoners (Jews and others) on a final death march to Germany.

Five other death camps also existed: Lublin, Treblinka, Belzec, Sobibor, and Kulmhof. These other camps had few, if any, survivors. These six extermination camps were the scenes of the last phase of the Final Solution.

The Burden of Survival

One survivor, an Italian chemist and writer named Primo Levi, had worked in the Resistance in Italy during the war. One day in February 1944, he was suddenly arrested by the Nazis, and shipped by box-car with many others to Auschwitz in Poland. When he arrived, the number 174517 was tattooed on his arm, and he became part of a work detail. He became one of the gaunt, lifeless men he saw when he arrived, walking with a stiff shuffle and a beaten look. Over the gate of Auschwitz hung a sign: "Arbeit macht frei"—Work makes [one] free—a grim joke.

The experience left a deep mark on Levi, and he spent the rest of his life writing and speaking about his experiences and the Holocaust. He wanted to make sure that people understood what it was like and what it meant about human beings and what they could sink to. He described what it was like to be pushed to incredible fatigue, and what it was like not to know whether loved ones were well, or tortured, or dead. Guards might herd them into a shower room and leave them for hours while they stood in their bare feet in cold water, or they might march them to the gas chamber. The prisoners never knew what would happen next.[10]

Toward the end of his life, Levi became discouraged because some groups of German historians had begun to write revisionist histories of what happened to the Jews in Germany during the Holocaust. Other countries, they said, had committed genocide, and therefore it was not so uncommon. The Soviets, for example, had waged internal wars against political enemies. That was also genocide, they said. Other analysts claimed that the Holocaust had never happened.[11] Discouraged and depressed, Levi, who had always retained his trust in humanity, apparently committed suicide in April 1987.[12] Forty-three years had passed since his train ride through the night to the horrors of Auschwitz.

Stages of Genocide

In the story of the Holocaust we can see all the steps or stages of genocide that appear in both Armenia and Rwanda. We will also see many similar steps in the stories of Cambodia and the former Yugoslavia. How genocide proceeds:

- A group of victims is set apart by the society surrounding them. A negative stereotype becomes established and people readily believe that members of this group are different.

- Ordinary people may begin to discriminate against this group and even attack them.

- The marked group loses many or all legal rights.

- Physical and social isolation of the target group begins.

- Politicians and the media begin to characterize the marked group as less than human. They are called names, such as "cockroaches," or "riffraff," or they are referred to in other dehumanizing ways. Finally, influenced by this attitude, ordinary people begin to think of the target group in this way.

- An event triggers the genocide. The event may be the start of a war, or an assassination, such as the 1938 assassination of a German embassy official.

- Those who commit genocide come to believe their actions are morally right, and the genocide continues.[13]

3

The Holocaust: Why?

"We have the moral right, we had the duty to our people to do it; to kill this people who would kill us."

—Heinrich Himmler, head of the SS, referring to the Jews in a speech, 1943[1]

At the end of World War II, the Allied soldiers who found the camps filled with victims were filled with horror. They confronted the evidence of unthinkable deeds. Piles of human ashes stood next to ovens that had been used to destroy corpses. They found heaps of jewelry, gold teeth, watches, clothing, and other loot the Nazis had salvaged from their victims. Unburied corpses awaited cremation or mass burial. Horribly malnourished prisoners who knew they were meant to be next looked with gaunt faces and glazed eyes at this new set of soldiers.

How could human beings have done these things to other human beings?

The Nazis' Final Solution was part of a master plan to achieve an ideology: supremacy of the "Master Race," as they thought of themselves. The steps they took to achieve their goals are seen again and again in other genocides. Central to the process is the systematic extermination of a specific group of people.

Some people call genocide "murder by government." It is always planned and deliberate. Almost always that plan is organized, promoted, and carried out by those in power. However, without the support of the general public, they could not succeed.

Gaining the Right to Destroy

Those in power can get ordinary people to agree to otherwise unthinkable mass killings. To do this, they use a combination of devices, including brainwashing, mass media, and group think—people's natural tendency to be influenced by others. Existing hatreds and long-held alienation between people of different backgrounds are the propagandists' biggest assets. They capitalize on fear of the Other. The Nazis used several of these weapons to gain the right to destroy.

Milieu of Existing Hatred

Existing anti-Semitism helped Hitler and the SS harness the energy of the Germans and direct it toward their political goals.

Dehumanization of the Targets

Virtually every perpetrator of genocide has relied on a range of verbal and physical techniques for making the target people seem subhuman. The Jews were "vermin," according to Hitler. He promoted this idea, used laws to lend it authority, and marked all Jews with a yellow Star of David.

Hiding Behind Paper Shuffling

Much of the Holocaust's machinery was hidden behind the screen of bureaucratic paper shuffling. There were forms to fill out and reports to be filed. The details passed through the hands of civil servants without notice. Even to those participating, the process seemed normal and the end results unexamined. And for most Germans, life remained normal until World War II.

Evil as Ordinary

Soon the Holocaust machinery became so much a part of everyday events that what would ordinarily strike people as unthinkable atrocities came to seem ordinary. Hitler used expressions that hid their true meaning, such as Final Solution, to refer to violence inflicted on victims. This trick keeps people from seeing that the process is evil.

Group Mentality and Momentum

Psychological studies show that one of the most effective tools of genocide is the sense of belonging and group participation. Participants also develop a sense of a chain of events that must be kept going. This commitment to continue what was begun actually becomes more important than other considerations.

As happened with the Order Police Battalion 101, peer pressure plays a large factor in keeping people from straying from a group action.

The Veil of War

War creates an atmosphere of unreality and departure from the norm, and under this veil, many heinous crimes may go unchecked. Most genocides occur amid the mayhem of war, and this is no accident. Not until World War II began did Hitler begin to exterminate the Jews, and the Final Solution began halfway through the conflict.

Sadism and the Thirst for Personal Power

Some Nazi killers and torturers actually took pleasure in what they did. They gained a sense of power over their victims, a sense of togetherness and strength from belonging to a group that dominated another group.

The Human Crime

People tend to cling to what they know and to fear the unknown, the Other. Humans are the only species to carry out systematic killing of the feared Other. Leo Kuper wrote in *Genocide: Its Political Use in the 20th Century*, "Though animals do engage in intra-species killing, genocide is essentially a human crime."[2]

Bodies of dead inmates at the Gestapo camp of Lager Nordhausen. This photo shows less than half of those who died of starvation there or were shot by Gestapo police.

When people talk about genocide, words such as "barbaric," "insane," or "animalistic" are often used, but these words sidestep issues of responsibility. They make genocide into something that only abnormal, ignorant, or ill-bred people would do.

But education does not prevent the crime of genocide. Germany probably had the most highly educated population in the world at the time of the Holocaust. Pol Pot, who led the Cambodian genocide in the 1970s, received seventeen years of education from the French government, including several years in Paris. Hitler may have been insane—his writings and speeches were filled with paranoia, hatred, and unhinged thinking—but he was elected to office and supported by the German people. Certainly not all those who followed him, committed atrocities, or allowed them to take place could have been insane.

Genocide is also not animalistic, or even the work of primitive, uncivilized humans. We may try to blame genocides on our animal instincts, but in the end we have to face the fact that the crime is uniquely human.

"In fact," writes Roger W. Smith, professor of government at William and Mary College, "all of these labels are ways of evading a recognition that ordinary human beings have a capacity for destroying their fellows when caught up in certain political and social conditions." Smith points out that genocide requires three important ingredients that only humans have: sustained organization, rationalization, and elaborate cover-up.[3]

Organized Crime

Genocide cannot take place without planning and careful execution. It is deliberate and systematic. Thousands, even millions, of victims are involved. Planning such a large undertaking is a momentous task. Victims have to be transported long distances. Willing executioners must be present and equipped, and there must be enough of them. Mass graves must be dug.

The purpose behind genocide is irrational, but the

process of achieving it is carefully calculated. In the twentieth century, technology became important for the first time. Radio, television, public address systems, and other communications technology have made it possible to stir people to action. Railways made possible the transportation of thousands of Jews to extermination sites.

Rationalized Crime

Human beings have a sense of moral right, so a rationale has to be created. The executioners and the rest of the genocidal society have to have reasons they can give themselves to explain why what they are doing must be all right. This process is known as rationalization—the process of creating reasonable-sounding explanations to replace real explanations that are less acceptable, socially or politically. This process is uniquely human.

Crime Covered Up

International criticism and political pressures from other countries become likely, if genocide occurs out in the open. So, when a government commits genocide, it will always try to cover up the crime. In 1915, Turks and Kurds force-marched more than a million Armenians to their deaths. International observers saw what they were doing, but felt helpless to stop them because the nations of the world were in the middle of World War I. Later, the Turkish government went to some pains to deny the events and their origin at the central government level.

Armenian Genocide: The Denial of Mass Murder

"Who, after all, speaks today of the annihilation of the Armenians?"

—Adolf Hitler[1]

In 1915, nearly all Armenians living in what is now Turkey were forced from their homes by soldiers. They had only one or two days' notice before beginning a long, agonizing march to relocation in the Syrian desert. On the way, they had little or no water or food. Their clothes became tattered and their shoes wore out. Marauders attacked them and took what little they had been able to bring with them. "In a few days," one observer wrote, "what had

45

been a procession of normal human beings became a stumbling horde of dust-covered skeletons, ravenously looking for scraps of food. . . ."[2] They died by the thousands along the way, of starvation, dehydration, and exhaustion. Some were beaten with clubs and bayonets. When they arrived, there was no place to stay, no food, no way of subsisting. Observers described what they saw with words like "piteous" and "hideous." They knew they had witnessed the slaughter of an entire nation. But today, the Turkish government denies that it ever happened.

Background

Armenians had lived for thousands of years in Armenia, a small, ancient region in western Asia and Anatolia, which makes up most of the country we now know as Turkey. In 1915, most of this traditional Armenian homeland was part of the Ottoman Empire, governed by Turks. The Armenians followed the Christian religion but were surrounded by a group of people who believed in Islam. Some authorities on genocide think that this tension alone was enough to inspire hatred and murder. Persecution had become commonplace, and Armenians endured atrocities and repression for centuries at the hands of the Ottoman sultans. In 1895, a massacre authorized by Sultan Habdul Hamid killed three hundred thousand Armenians, followed by another massacre in 1909. An atmosphere of hatred and mistrust was pervasive.

Meanwhile, some Armenians lived in nearby Russia, a longtime enemy of the Ottoman Empire, and served as volunteers in the tsar's army during various conflicts, adding to the Turks' hatred and anger.

In 1915, the Young Turk political party took over the government of the Ottoman Empire. These radical young men had new ideas for modernizing the empire and "purifying" its people.

In February 1915, Armenians serving in the Turkish army were stripped of their arms and positions and expelled from the military. Soon afterward prominent Armenians at the local level were arrested. The order went out for able-bodied Armenian men to report to local authorities; most were executed.

By April, the deportations began. Women and children were grouped into caravans and herded across Anatolia to the Syrian desert. On the way, the Ottoman police and local citizens repeatedly attacked

Orphaned Armenian children in the region of the Syrian desert after deportations and murders by the Ottoman government in 1915.

the caravans. They raped and killed their victims and stole their property. Families were split up. Women were forced to convert to Islam, and many were forced into slavery. The caravans had no leaders (they had been arrested) and no young men (they had been executed) and no weapons. They were compelled to journey deep into the desert, where there was no food. Only three hundred thousand reached safety in Russia. The rest died or were sold into slavery. In the end, no one remained in his or her former homeland.

The Importance of Remembering

After the Holocaust, a series of international trials held in Nuremberg, Germany, revealed the details of the Nazi genocide. No such trial ever took place for the Young Turks. Today's Turkish government claims that the massacres never happened. They even choose to ignore the documentation made at the time by historians, diplomats, journalists, and photographers, because no legal action was ever brought against the Young Turks. It was quickly forgotten by most of the world.

The Genocide That Did Not Happen

The denial of the massacres has had a powerful impact on history. When people try to rewrite or retell history, their revised story is called a revisionist history. Of course, historians sometimes find facts or frame new interpretations in later years that cast the past in a new light. But people also often forget or ignore portions of history that reflect badly on themselves.

According to historian Richard G. Hovannisian, "The history of the denial of the Armenian Genocide has passed through several phases, each somewhat different in emphasis but all characterized by efforts to avoid responsibility and the moral, material, and political consequences of admission."[3] At first, the Turks tried to hide their plans for the Armenians from international visitors. As the caravans of refugees began to stream across the countryside and that was no longer possible, the Turks began to justify their actions. The Armenians, they said, had brought these actions upon themselves. But international disapproval began to build. Turkey's allies were not happy. Neutral countries tried to intercede. Britain, France, and Russia announced that they were holding the Turkish government responsible.

However, later, after the war ended in 1918, the Turkish government that came to power at that time denounced the Young Turks and claimed that the Armenians were Russian allies. Justifying the deportations as necessary action against an internal enemy in time of war, the new Turkish authorities at the same time did denounce the Young Turks' "policy of extermination and robbery."[4] These, they suggested, were criminal actions committed by an "unnatural government" but certainly not the fault of the Turks. And, they said, further blame could be placed with Turkey's former allies, the Germans.

From exile, one member of the Young Turks government insisted that no plan for extermination ever existed, although he admitted that some officials had abused their authority and many innocent people had suffered as a result.

Weighing the Facts

Which of these stories is true? As Hovannisian points out, the "many well-intentioned individuals who believe that . . . there are always two sides to a story" end up giving equal weight to both sides.[5] But both sides of a story are not always equally believable.

In *Clear Thinking: A Practical Introduction*, former science teacher Hy Ruchlis points out that it is easy not to think clearly about many "facts" we encounter in daily life. One reason is that wrong or deceptive information often parades as fact:

> Any statement claimed to be a fact cannot be accepted as true until it is verified in some objective way. That is, the observer should remain unemotional, unbiased, and unprejudiced (impartial) when evaluating the truth or falsity of what are reported to be "facts." These facts should be verified in some reliable way, through gathering of information, observation, or testing.[6]

But how can anyone achieve an objective view of an issue as emotional as genocide? Much is at stake on both sides, and the cases made by both sides are highly emotional. The Turkish say nothing happened. The Turkish government fears that the former Ottoman Empire may be required to compensate Armenian survivors. Turkey has become respected for its political and economic strength and its culture. Turkey also has spent decades overcoming the stereotype of the terrible Turk.

Armenians, meanwhile, feel deep frustration at the erasure of this part of their ethnic story. In 1980, a motion was defeated in the United States Congress to set aside April 24 as a day of remembrance for the victims and survivors of the Armenian genocide. To the Armenians, this is proof that Turkish influence and political priorities have warped American policy. To partisans of the Turks, it shows that perhaps there is another side to the story.

Massive amounts of documentation support the Armenian case. The massacre of the Armenians is well documented by people who were neither Turks nor Armenians, as shown by sociologist Leo Kuper in his article, "The Turkish Genocide of Armenians, 1915–1917."[7]

Simple denial is not enough in the face of such overwhelming wrongdoing.

The Beginning of Modern Genocide

Genocide is an ancient crime, probably as old as human existence. Yet, genocide in the twentieth century had some deadly new aspects that made it in many ways even more horrible than before. Advances in communications, weapons, and efficiency 3made possible the killing of many more people in a shorter period of time. The Armenian genocide was the first to gain momentum from these modern technologies. "The Turkish massacres and 'deportations' of the Armenians were the most notable early example of the employment of modern communications and technology in the acting out and realization of political violence," wrote Michael J. Arlen in *Passage to Ararat*, his classic work on the Armenian genocide.[8]

The methods used in the Armenian genocide also show a new understanding of human psychology. Powerful psychological techniques were used to undermine victims. These techniques have come back to haunt us over and over again.

- People were split up to weaken their resolve and reduce their psychological strength.

- Leaders were separated from the group and eliminated.

- Able-bodied men were removed from the community to weaken and demoralize those who remained.

- The weak and ill, those least likely to fight back or survive, were victimized.

- Those who could be used in some way— women who would convert to Islam rather than starve; people who could serve as slaves—were separated from the rest.

- The victims were demoralized through harassment and loss.

This overarching plan, like the Nazis' Final Solution, could not have succeeded without the approval and collaboration of ordinary citizens. The plan would have failed if the Young Turks had not had the cooperation of the territories through which the caravans of victims passed. The government had to be able to count upon the citizens of those areas to approve the deportation, not to interfere, and to help harass the victims.

Was It Genocide?

The objective of the Young Turks was to completely erase the presence of the people known as Armenians. As a result, as many as 1.2 million Armenians disappeared from the Ottoman Empire between May and August 1915. A few escaped to Russia. Some remained in the urban areas of Constantinople (modern Istanbul) and Smyrna. All the rest died.

Perhaps the most chilling and telling sign of genocide was the systematic murder of Armenian children. That crime shows that the Turks wanted to be sure that this enemy would never haunt them again.

Children lay dead or dying along the path of the Armenian refugees, where their tormentors had murdered them or their mothers were forced to leave them behind, 1915–1916.

5

Cambodia: A People Turned on Itself

"When it rains in Cambodia the water washes away mud, exposing more of Pol Pot's mass graves."

—Lindsay Murdoch, journalist[1]

The nightmare in Cambodia began in 1975, with the ironic goal of creating an economic utopia. In the end, millions of people suffered torture, were murdered, or starved to death in the name of this vision.

Background

Cambodia is a small country on the Gulf of Thailand, where heavy forests dominate most of the low-lying countryside. To the east lies Vietnam, with Laos and Thailand to the north. Ninety percent of the population of Cambodia is Khmer, and Khmer is the country's official language. The Khmer people probably traveled south to this region from China long ago. The remaining 10 percent of the country's population is Chinese and Vietnamese.

During Cambodia's early history, the Khmer Empire included regions now located within the boundaries of Laos, Vietnam, and Thailand. However, it began to decline after about the mid-fifteenth century. By 1863, Cambodia had become a French protectorate. In 1887, Cambodia was colonized by France as part of the Union of Indochina. That relationship ended briefly with an invasion by Japan during World War II, but after the war, in 1945, France reclaimed Cambodia. However, nationalist parties influenced King Norodom Sihanouk to press for independence, which the country gained six years later, in 1951.

Southeast Asia had seen considerable strife during French rule, and conflicts in the region continued after the French left in 1954. Agreements made at the Geneva conferences forced withdrawal of the Indochina Communist Party to North Vietnam in 1954, but fighting broke out again in 1956 as South Vietnam attempted to repulse advances from the north. Sihanouk turned over his throne to his father in 1955, but remained prince of Cambodia, prime minister, head of the chief political party, and later, head of state. He hoped to steer Cambodia clear of involvement in the Vietnam conflict by aligning with

China and allowing North Vietnam to launch attacks from the Cambodian seacoast.

Meanwhile, more trouble began brewing as a new Communist party formed and grew in secret, beginning in 1960. Under its leader, Pol Pot, the party would become known as the Khmer Rouge, or the Communist Party of Cambodia. By 1968 it had gained sufficient military strength to stage armed attacks on the Cambodian government.

South Vietnam and the United States bombed interior regions of Cambodia in an effort to wipe out North Vietnamese pockets in 1969–1970. When peace finally came to Vietnam in 1975, though, Cambodia continued to suffer attacks from the Khmer Rouge. Finally, in 1975, the capital city of Phnom Penh fell to the Khmer Rouge. Now, most Cambodians expected they would have peace at last. Surely what followed would be better than the continual battering they had endured for the past five years. Now, they thought, they would be able to rebuild their country.

They were wrong.

Years of Terror

A week after the Khmer Rouge took power, city dwellers were rounded up and forced to leave their homes and their jobs. They were ordered into the countryside to farm. The city streets emptied. The roads of Cambodia were filled with people walking long distances, unsure of where they were going. Often they hoped to reach relatives living on distant farms who might take them in. Some faced a monthlong journey on foot. Many died on the road in the weeks that followed, especially the old and the very young. Later, many more died of starvation or were killed in random executions.

As one survivor explained, the Khmer Rouge told city dwellers to leave their homes to avoid being bombed by the Americans. "We were confused and intimidated," explained Thida B. Mam years later. That is how Cambodia became, as she put it, "a nation of homeless refugees overnight." It had been a trick, but the victims realized that too late. The Khmer Rouge gained absolute power of the entire population of Phnom Penh by stripping them of everything and making them dependent on the Khmer Rouge for food, information, and daily existence.[2]

Pol Pot in the Cambodian jungle.

The Khmer Rouge called these former city dwellers the "new people." Newcomers to the revolution, they would always be suspect. The farmer peasants, in whose name the revolution had been won, were called the "base people."

With the cities emptied, the new regime began to transform the Cambodian social structure. The communist government did away with money, markets, and private property. The Khmer Rouge also closed all the schools and universities. Intellectuals were automatically under suspicion, and people who wore glasses (a sign of urban sophistication and intellectualism) were often arrested and imprisoned or executed. Western medicine was outlawed. Buddhist monasteries were closed.

Civil freedoms were curtailed, including freedom of movement. Publishing of any kind was forbidden. People could not even write a letter and mail it—the postal system no longer existed. People were not allowed to indulge in leisure activities—no ball games, dances, or amusements. Everyone was expected to wear identical plain, black cotton clothes. Those who disobeyed were dealt with severely. A repeat offender could expect to be thrown into one of the Khmer Rouge's deadly prisons, or executed. Many were killed without apparent reason.

Work was assigned by the revolutionary organization, which now claimed to be the "mother and father" of everyone. City dwellers were sent into the fields. Thida Mam recalls working in the fields during the "killing season of 1978." She tells the story of how a village leader came on his bicycle and took his fifteen-year-old niece from where she was working next to Mam. Angka Loeu (The Organization), he said, was relocating the girl and her mother. Mam knew that he really meant he was escorting his relatives to their extermination. Other coworkers hung themselves in despair. Each day, she trembled to see any leader from the village. She tried to be inconspicuous. "How do you explain a fear that swallows you like quicksand?" she asked, looking back.[3]

Prison S-21

For years, no one knew where Pol Pot, the dictatorial leader of this radical revolution, came from or even his real name. He was ambitious for power, and this drove much of the character of the revolution. Purges wracked the countryside beginning in 1977, and thousands were killed. Pol Pot personally called for the torture and execution of nearly fourteen thousand individuals he believed were his enemies. They were arrested and thrown into prison in a dungeon known by the code name S-21. Most of them were later shown to be loyal party members.

A Misguided Revolution

The Khmer Rouge had misunderstood the needs of the rural poor in whose name they acted. They also mis-judged the economic effects of their policies and their country's interdependence on surrounding countries. At one level, though, it was an idealistic effort to make big changes very quickly. In the words of one

Young children look away from skulls at the "Killing Fields" memorial in Phnom Penh, Cambodia.

historian, "No other regime tried to go so quickly or so far. No other inflicted as many casualties on the country's population."[4] It proved to be a deadly combination—one that resulted in millions of deaths.

The Lucky Few

Only the lucky ones managed to survive, and a few managed to leave Cambodia, such as Heang Eap and her husband, Hwai Eap. They succeeded in escaping with their baby girl, Sopagna, even though Heang Eap was gravely malnourished at the time she gave birth, and had no milk for the baby.

Sopagna's parents were both living in Phnom Penh when the Khmer Rouge took over, but they did not know each other. Along with everyone else, they were compelled to set out for the unknown countryside. They met each other in a rural village where the Khmer Rouge forced them into slave labor, working in the fields. Neither one ever saw their parents after they were forced to separate from them as they left the city on April 17, 1975. Both of Sopagna's grandparents were killed by the Khmer Rouge, and so were most of her aunts and uncles.

Today, Sopagna is a teenager in San Francisco. She and her younger brother, Robert, are cross-country track stars for their school. She knows, though, how lucky she and her parents were to have survived. On a visit to Cambodia with her mother, she met an uncle who told her how her grandfather died. So starved he could not walk, he used a stick to pull himself to the village kitchen. There, he begged to be given some food, even just a bowl of rice. He was refused. Slowly, he crept back to his living quarters, where he had found shelter with other "new people" who had been thrown out of the cities. There, he died of starvation. Thousands of others shared his fate.[5]

Auto-Genocide

Some experts call these events that occurred in Cambodia an auto-genocide—a systematic massacre of its own people by its own government. Technically, the groups wiped out by the Khmer Rouge did not fit any category listed in the UN definition of genocide. Yet, from 1975 to 1979, the Khmer Rouge massacred between 1 and 2.5 million Cambodians. Many of the earmarks of genocide existed in Cambodia during these years, and because of the horrendous outcome, this story is included.

The Khmer Rouge leadership attempted to eliminate dissident groups through a three-step process. First, they isolated each group by legally prohibiting the existence of its members. Groups marked for this treatment included Buddhist monks, ethnic minorities, and all those considered tainted by "feudal," "bourgeois," or "foreign" influences. Second, they disbanded the group and sent its members to separate destinations. Third, they physically destroyed the group's members. Leaders and those who resisted disbanding were killed. Others were deliberately subjected to extreme cruelty, which ended in death. Forced starvation and disease wiped out these segments of the population. Medical personnel who might have helped them were executed.

The result was a human tragedy of immense proportions. Sometimes people say, "Follow your own conscience." But Hitler believed he was doing the right thing for Germany and the German people. Pol Pot and his followers probably believed that what they were doing was right. If there is a lesson to learn here, it may be that what "feels right" is not always right.

End of the Road

In 1979, the Vietnamese army advanced on Cambodia, and the Khmer Rouge fled. When the members of the revolutionary organization took flight, they took hundreds of thousands of Cambodian civilians along with them. When this massive group

A Canadian medic with the United Nations Transitional Authority in Cambodia (UNTAC) in 1993 helps an elderly man damaged by the effects of starvation.

arrived at the Thailand border, there was no food for such an enormous crowd of displaced persons. International humanitarian groups came to the rescue with food and aid. Many innocent people were saved from starvation. However, the Khmer Rouge also were saved and sustained, so they could come back another day. They were able to strengthen their forces and return later to wage another ten years of conflict. The nightmare continued, ironically, because good people came to their aid.

That happened again during the 1990s in Rwanda. However, by the end of the century, humanitarians had begun to try to sort out perpetrators from victims when giving aid. At the end of the conflict in Kosovo in the Balkan countries in 1999, the United States and its NATO allies refused economic aid to Serbia. That was because its leader was Slobodan Milosevic, a man indicted for genocide by the International Criminal Tribunal for the former Yugoslavia.

Pol Pot died of heart failure in April 1998. Today, a memorial in Phnom Penh, the Cambodian capital, honors those who died there during Pol Pot's reign. An elected democratic government replaced the dictatorship of Pol Pot. UN aides are helping Cambodians disarm mines still found in the fields. At last, this chapter of history seems to be over.

For Thida Mam, Heang and Hwai Eap, and many others, though, the memories remain. And no one will ever know what contributions the world lost when the lives of 2 million people were cut short.

6

Rwanda: Incited Massacre

In 1994, the roads of Rwanda were crowded with people fleeing for their lives. By the hundreds and thousands, they streamed across the borders of their tiny country into nearby Tanzania, Zaire (now Democratic Republic of Congo), and Burundi. Behind them, adults and children were attacking their neighbors with machetes. They left the dead bodies of mutilated babies on doorsteps. They cut off the heads of women, children, and men. They cut out their intestines. They left bodies in heaps in churchyards and village streets. Before it was over, more than one million Tutsi victims had died at the hands of Hutu attackers. By 1994, hundreds of thousands of Tutsi refugees crowded into camps across the border in Zaire, unable to return to their homeland.

Rwanda and its Different Peoples

Rwanda is a small country in the middle of Africa's Great Lakes region. Long ago, the dark-skinned people known as the Hutu who settled Rwanda were joined by a smaller group, the Tutsi. The Tutsi were taller, leaner, and lighter skinned. They arrived so long ago, though, that by now many Tutsi and Hutu have intermarried, and in some cases many of the physical differences have disappeared. There is also a third, much smaller group of shorter people, the Twa. All these groups speak the same language and share the same culture. Rwanda is rare among African nations because its citizens are not divided by different cultures.

For a long time, the Tutsi and Hutu lived side by side in peace, but the Tutsi usually held positions of power. The king was Tutsi, and so was his court. The Tutsi owned cattle, a symbol of wealth. The Hutu often worked for Tutsi landowners. Despite differences of status, the Hutu and Tutsi worked out a peaceful arrangement. As journalist Philip Gourevitch put it, "until . . . 1959 there had never been systematic political violence recorded between Hutus and Tutsis—anywhere."[1]

Yet the shared culture and language did not prevent hatred from taking root and growing to monstrous proportions in the mid-twentieth century.

Colonial Legacy

Much responsibility for the divisions among Tutsi and Hutu lies with Belgian colonists who arrived in 1916 and took over the country. The colonists placed the Tutsi in positions of power over the Hutu, taking advantage of a social structure that seemed to exist before. This appeared to work well, but in 1959, the moderate, stable three-decade rule of Tutsi King Kigari V came to an end with his death. More ethnocentric Tutsi took charge, and their unfair policies caused widespread rebellions by Hutu, who wanted equal rights. Tens of thousands of Tutsi were killed. Colonial authorities shifted their support from the Tutsi, thinking the country's impending independence would be more stable under Hutu rule. In 1961, a Hutu government took over, put an end to the Tutsi monarchy, and declared Rwanda an independent republic.

Political power now lay with those who had been poor and hungry. These people were angry, often justifiably, about the way they had been treated in the past. Now they were also powerful. Massacres broke out almost immediately after independence was declared. Some twenty thousand Tutsi died, and another one hundred thousand fled for refuge to nearby countries. The country was ruled primarily by Hutu from the central region.

Ethnic violence increased steadily, until another Hutu faction, from northern Rwanda, staged a bloodless coup in 1973 that put Major-General Juvénal Habyarimana in power. The government shifted from military rule to civilian rule by 1975, and Habyarimana was elected president in 1978 and again in 1980. Many internal divisions plagued his government, and in 1989–1990, a huge drop in coffee prices caused deep damage to the nation's fragile agricultural economy. Political crisis followed.

In October 1990, from outside Rwandan borders, exiled Tutsi began a guerrilla invasion in the north. Hutus were outraged, and they used the attacks as an excuse to lash out at Tutsi still living within Rwanda. But in August 1993, a peace accord was signed that gave Tutsi and Hutu equal say in the government. Rebellious groups among the Hutu were not happy, however. On April 6, 1994, both President Habyarimana and the president of Burundi, Cyprien Ntaryamira, were killed when their plane was hit by a missile attack just outside the presidential palace in Kigali, Rwanda. That is when even greater troubles began. Angry Hutu blamed the Tutsi for the "traitorous" attack. In fact, many observers think that Hutu extremists staged the attack, removing the moderate Habyarimana and providing an excuse for punishing the Tutsi. Immediately, highly organized massacres of Tutsi and moderate Hutu began. Graves had already been prepared.

Campaign of Hate

By 1993, the United Nations had recognized Rwanda as a trouble spot and had placed twenty-five hundred peacekeeping troops in Rwanda as part of the UN Assistance Mission for Rwanda (UNAMIR). But these

Refugees wait to cross the bridge from Rwanda into Zaire (now the Democratic Republic of Congo), August 1994.

troops were not given authority to stop the violence. As conditions in Rwanda worsened, the United Nations actually pulled most of the peacekeepers out of the area, leaving only 270 peacekeepers in place.[2] Before long, even those were withdrawn. At the same time, several countries, including the United States, had experienced a disastrously unsuccessful peacekeeping mission in Western Somalia in 1993. Eighteen soldiers had died, and nothing the would-be peacemakers had done really helped. Wary from this experience, these countries were now reluctant to get involved in Rwanda. Evidence showed that the United Nations had full warning that genocide was about to take place. Yet, blocked by the nations that opposed intervention, the United Nations apparently could do nothing to help.

Boutros Boutros-Ghali, former secretary-general of the United Nations, said:

> Setbacks have occurred where traditional peacekeeping operations have been deployed to deal with war-like situations. Where cease-fires were not respected. Where cooperation of the parties was limited and sporadic. Where the perception of impartiality was difficult to maintain, as peacekeepers were required to perform limited enforcement tasks, for their own and others' protection. In Somalia and Bosnia, the world has seen the dangers of giving peace-keepers enforcement tasks.[3]

Then, in April 1994, a carefully structured campaign of massacres began. A state-controlled radio station, Mille Collines, played pop songs mixed with hate messages. Commentators called upon Hutus to "kill the Tutsi cockroaches." Announcers read lists of Tutsi names. Within days, many of these named citizens were killed.

In village after village, Hutus hunted down Tutsi in their homes or in the streets and stabbed them with machetes. Schoolteachers killed their own students. Churches were used as killing grounds. The seething hatred seemed uncontrollable.

Within one hundred days in 1994, eight hundred thousand Tutsi died at the hands of the Hutu, at a rate of some five thousand or more per day.

Massive Exodus and Death

Meanwhile, Tutsi exiles, who had fled to neighboring Uganda, returned to stage an invasion. They defeated the Hutu army and militia and captured Kigali, the capital. Some 1.7 million Hutu fled to nearby Zaire, Tanzania, and Burundi. Nearly as many were probably displaced within Rwanda. The upheaval was immense, and many died.

In July 1994 alone, fifty thousand Hutu who had taken shelter in eastern Zaire died there of disease, including dysentery, cholera, and dehydration.

Within the camps, members of the brutal Interahamwe militia (composed primarily of extremist Hutus) and the former Rwandan army were mixed in among the rest of the refugees. They were armed, and they continued to stir up trouble and dominate life in the camps. Here, too, humanitarian groups offered aid to those carrying out the genocide,

Many refugees were wounded and urgently needed medicine.

much as they had been forced to do in Cambodia. Appeals for help were ignored by the international community. As the government of Zaire began to force Rwandans to return home, Hutu forces staged an attack on Rwanda's new Tutsi government. Not until the Canadian government offered to lead a multinational force in 1996 did any other nation offer to help.

As it happened, though, just at that time, a group of Tutsi from Zaire forced the Interahamwe militia members out of the refugee camps, and the Hutu who had been under their control streamed back into

Rwanda. So, with the need removed, the multinational force was never used.

Speaking of these events in remarks during a visit to Rwanda in 1999, U.S. President Bill Clinton stated that, "we did not act quickly enough after the killing began. We should not have allowed the refugee camps to become safe havens for the killers. We did not immediately call these crimes by their rightful name: genocide."[4] As with the Holocaust, Armenia, and Cambodia, in Rwanda's hour of need, no one lifted a hand to help. When help did come, it was a case of too little, too late.

Victims of Fear and the Hunger for Power

In 1998, the United Nations International Criminal Tribunal for Rwanda handed down the first genocide sentence by an international court in condemnation of former Rwandan prime minister Jean Kambanda, who handed out weapons to Hutu civilians in 1994 to hunt down and kill "Tutsi cockroaches." Beginning in April 1994, Hutu militia and civilians murdered some five hundred thousand Tutsi neighbors and citizens, primarily with machetes and knives. It is generally considered one of the worst massacres of the twentieth century.

Behind these genocides lies a complex history. The long-standing social structure had broken down with nothing to replace it. And a buildup of mass fear and hatred allowed power-hungry leaders from both groups to stir up a frenzy of murder to serve their own self-interest.

Some of the 250,000 refugees who fled to Tanzania in one twenty-four-hour period.

Hatred Returns

It is not all over: In late 1997, the hate radio began again. The Mille Collines radio station seemed to have sprung back to life, this time named Voice of the Patriot. Broadcasting from a mobile transmitter across the border in Congo, the announcer urged Hutus within Rwanda to "rise as one to combat Tutsis." Within a few days 272 Tutsi in Rwanda were dead. They were victims of attacks by Hutu rebels who left behind propaganda promoting similar anti-Tutsi hate messages. Later, the radio station was heard broadcasting from Tanzania, on the other side of Rwanda, making the signal difficult to track down and stop.

The worst days were in 1994, but the killing in Rwanda has not yet ended. Even with the presence of the United Nations, killing continued to take place in 1998 and 1999.

Slow Recovery

Under a new government, Rwanda has recovered slowly. Before that, its infrastructure—bridges, roads, and buildings—were a shambles. Meanwhile, driven from the surrounding nations, some 2.8 million refugees poured back into Rwanda, where the total population was only about 5.5 to 6 million in 1995. That is a population increase of nearly 50 percent, a large increase in a country with poor resources and a struggling economy. Some of those returning had left as long ago as 1959, and others had left in 1994. All these people came back to demolished homes and wrecked villages. Rebuilding their lives will be a long, slow process.

That is also the case with the people living in the Balkan region of Eastern Europe, where war, genocide, and so-called ethnic cleansing have also produced vast groups of displaced people.

7

Bosnia and Kosovo: Genocide and "Ethnic Cleansing"

"Vengeance knows no bounds in Bosnia."

—Elizabeth Neuffler, journalist[1]

For the mountainous regions of Eastern Europe known as the Balkan countries, the 1990s brought violent times. Times of murder, pillage, and rape directed against minority religious groups. Times of torture and forced exodus from homes. Times of revenge and retaliation. Times of war, bombing, and destruction. A fragile peace would be negotiated in one area only to be brutally broken in another.

In the bitter winter of 1999, just as peace efforts were beginning to succeed in nearby Bosnia-Herzegovina, massacres began to occur in Kosovo, a small province in Serbia. A minority group there, the ethnic Albanians, had begun to break away from Serbia to form an independent country. This move threatened the power of the Serbian government and it awakened deep-seated religious hatred of the Moslem Albanians among Greek Orthodox Serbs who lived in Kosovo.

In January, attackers wearing black hoods and Yugoslav army and police uniforms entered the village of Racak and murdered forty-five ethnic Albanian villagers, including a child. On Saturday, January 16, U.S. Ambassador William Walker arrived. As head of a multinational team of peacekeepers who tried to oversee a negotiated cease-fire in Kosovo, he came to the village in answer to reports of the murders. There he saw more than twenty corpses lying dead on a hillside, "most of them old men shot in the head at point-blank range." The others were found later.

Walker later told reporters in Racak, "Although I am not a lawyer, from what I personally saw, I do not hesitate to describe the event as a massacre, obviously a crime very much against humanity."[2]

One of the women of the village, Sandije Ramadani, tearfully told journalists that she had taken refuge in a locked basement with twenty-five other women and their children. From their hideout, she said, they heard the men screaming. "It sounded like animals," she said. She later found her brother, dead. Others also found loved ones among the dead. One man found his brother's body without a head.[3]

The Former Yugoslavia

Some people call this region of Eastern Europe the "former Yugoslavia" because, under the leadership of Yugoslav Communist Party leader Josip Broz Tito, the countries in this area were combined under one strong government from 1946 until Tito's death in May 1980.

Without Tito, though, economic difficulties and conflicts among ethnic groups began to tear at the unification that had lasted nearly thirty-five years. The countries that had been bound together began to separate into independent states: Bosnia (or Bosnia-Herzegovina), Serbia, Croatia, Montenegro, Macedonia, and Slovenia. Now a group of small countries exist side by side, nestled among rugged mountains, where, in happier times, Olympic athletes plowed the slopes with their skis.

As the countries separated, unrest and violence grew. Animosities that had smoldered beneath the surface for years under Tito's communist regime now ignited, and old hatreds boiled over. Brutal conflicts broke out in a series of deep, wrenching struggles for ethnic domination of these areas.

By the 1990s, national military forces, guerrilla armies, and roaming paramilitary militia had made this region a bristling knot of overlapping struggles. As in Rwanda, neighbor was often pitted against neighbor.

Before the events in Kosovo in the late 1990s, warring factions in Bosnia-Herzegovina had dominated world attention. The situation was not just a

A Muslim woman in a state of shock and exhaustion after being forced to flee on foot with her baby from her home in Bosnia-Herzegovina.

conventional war to gain territory or put down an uprising. The tactics in this conflict had deep psychological undertones. The methods of persecution became known as "ethnic cleansing."

In Bosnia: Ethnic Cleansing

The war in Bosnia reminded many people of the persecution of Jews in Nazi Germany and the Nazi ideal of ethnic purity. It also recalled the many warring factions and attempts at "cleansing" in the Balkans during World War II. The unity under Tito after the war turned out to be just a brief relief from many old conflicts.

By the 1990s, the struggle for power had become vicious. Serb men raped Muslim and Croat women, slit the throats of neighbors, and sadistically tortured their prisoners. The atrocities that began in 1992 continued well into 1998 in an effort to frighten Muslims and Croats into leaving Bosnia to the Serbs. On all sides, propaganda and manipulation played an important part in heating hatred to the point of criminal violence and murder.

But, can these events be considered genocide? The line between genocide and other war crimes is not always easy to see. Humanitarian Alain Destexhe pointed out, rightly, that the motivation in the Balkans was not technically the same as in most genocide. The Serbs wanted to obtain territory held by Muslims and Croats. They killed, maimed, and destroyed to frighten people into leaving, not to exterminate them. However, many patterns seen in genocide appeared in Bosnia, with many of the same ghastly results.

Also, not everyone agrees with Destexhe. In a formal application filed with the International Court of Justice in the Hague in 1993, the government of Bosnia-Herzegovina contended that ethnic cleansing is in fact just a disguised program of genocide.[4] By the end of 1999, several Serbian officials had been indicted by an international tribunal with charges of crimes against humanity, including genocide.

As this boy's face shows, most Bosnian young people have suffered deeply from the conflicts. Many have lost family members and have endured shelling and shooting.

Srebrenica: One Story of Bosnia

In 1995, as international diplomats struggled to negotiate a peace in Bosnia, tragedy struck Muslims isolated in the city of Srebrenica. This town had been a supposedly safe area, set aside by agreement as a haven. In July 1995, Serb forces broke the agreement and overran the area. Muslims were to be transported out of the area by the Serb army, but many Muslims distrusted this arrangement. As in Armenia and Germany, the Serbs pulled men and boys aside, apparently marking them for death. A large group of about fifteen thousand fled through the woods, but they met with ambushes by the Serbs. Grenades, poison gas, and machine-gun fire rang through the forest, and many died.

Rifet Mujic was among those who made it through the forest. In April 1996, he told interviewers,

> When I counted later, 25 members of my close family, my nearest and dearest family, all gone. And that wounds me terribly. . . . I don't have the people I used to sit around with, the people I used to talk to. . . . Your house, buildings, or apartment, that can all be compensated for, but your family, never. It's lost forever. And now, let me tell you, I feel such grief that I don't know what to do with myself.[5]

The International Committee of the Red Cross (ICRC) received formal inquiries from relatives for at least six thousand people who were missing following the events at Srebrenica. Almost every Muslim displaced from Srebrenica in 1995 knew at least one person who was missing, most likely dead—and that was in just one city. In Bosnia-Herzegovina, the numbers in 1995 approached twenty-seven thousand missing people.

Many may be victims of war, not genocide. However, experts see strong evidence that many were victims of deliberate or arbitrary killings. One fifty-five-year-old man, Hurem Suljic, told how he and others were detained by Serbs at Potocari near Srebrenica. Some were beaten, and some were executed in the night. Then he was blindfolded and taken by bus with a group of others to a sports field, where they were made to stand in four rows. He heard automatic gunfire but was not hit. He hid himself among the dead bodies until the guards left, then struggled out and escaped with two other survivors.[6]

Another man, Drazen Erdemovic, a twenty-five-year-old soldier in the Bosnian Serb army, told of participating in a similar mass execution. This series of murders left approximately twelve hundred Muslims dead. Erdemovic said he and other soldiers took ten prisoners at a time to a field, lined them up facing away from the soldiers, and shot them. If any showed signs of life, the soldiers shot them again, in the head.[7]

As many as three thousand gravesites have been reported in Bosnia-Herzegovina. Observers believe that three hundred of those contain many bodies each.

In Kosovo: Forced Out at Gunpoint

The trouble in Kosovo did not break out until the spring of 1998, but the tensions were similar to those in Bosnia. Many residents of Kosovo wanted independence from Serbia. However, the campaign had been peacefully led by a popular pacifist, Ibrahim Rugova. A more aggressive band of guerrilla fighters existed, known as the Kosovo Liberation Army (KLA), but they were not widely supported at first.

Serbian president Slobodan Milosevic and other leaders in Belgrade needed assurance that Kosovo would not make a strong move for separation. So they launched a military offensive against Kosovo in the spring of 1998. That decision only strengthened the guerrillas and rallied the people behind them. Many young men were put out of work when farms and shops were destroyed by the Serb attacks, so they joined the guerrillas as fresh recruits.

From there, things got worse. The Serb security forces in Kosovo chose terrorism to combat the increased threat. In January 1999, they aligned with local police and militia, and massacres began in the villages.

The nations of the North Atlantic Treaty Organization (NATO) had been severely criticized for looking the other way while people died by the hundreds of thousands in Rwanda. Determined not to let another Rwanda occur, NATO warned the government in Belgrade that they would bomb Serbia if the massacres and atrocities continued.

When no progress was made toward peace, and human rights violations continued, bombing by NATO forces began in March 1999 to try to stop the Serb offensive. Bridges in Serbia were destroyed. Belgrade shook with the explosions. Bombers attempted to locate munitions warehouses and tanks to bomb, but the bombing did not go smoothly. Serb military forces were difficult to locate in the mountainous territory. When serious mistakes occurred and civilians were killed, NATO nations came under severe criticism. They hoped to force a change in policy without great

Refugees from Kosovo crossing the Macedonian border. Many were forced to leave their homes so quickly that they had no time to pack.

risk to the lives of their soldiers, and only as a last resort did they prepare to send in ground troops, who would be greatly at risk.

Serbia responded with increased pressure on the people of Kosovo. Beginning in March 1999, thousands of ethnic Albanians were ordered to leave their homes immediately or be shot. They left behind their houses, belongings, and, often, their loved ones. They fled to the borders, on foot or in any vehicle they could find, in the deadly cold winter. Mass graves were filled with those who refused to follow orders.

Slobodan Milosevic forced 740,000 ethnic

Albanians to leave Kosovo. Many fled over mountainous roads to nearby Albania, Montenegro, or Macedonia. At one point a spokesperson for the International Medical Corps stated, "As many as 600 refugees per hour are crossing at Blace [into Macedonia]."[8]

More than 340 Albanians are known to have been murdered, and the presence of mass graves suggests that many more were killed as well.

"My Heart Is Wounded"

Cameron McWhirter, a journalist for the *Cincinnati Enquirer*, visited the Balkan countries in 1996, and he talked to people there—ordinary people who once

Refugees from Kosovo seeking safety in Albania, April 1999.

lived in the apartments and worked in the office buildings. One woman, Hiba Hadzismajlovic, was a sixty-three-year-old grandmother. She spoke with tears in her eyes of loved ones who had left, who had gone out of her life. She was luckier than Rifet Mujic. Her family is not dead. But she knows she may never see her children and grandchildren again. "My heart is wounded," she said. As she spoke she tapped her chest. "And my soul doesn't have any medicine to forget." Her life now has a great *"praznoca* [emptiness]," she said. "I feel an emptiness in me always," she told the interpreter. "Sometimes, it's just an empty hole; other times it's full of so much pain I can't stand it."[9]

For many people who have fled Bosnia-Herzegovina and Kosovo, and for many more who live there still, the pain and loss may never lessen.

8

Genocide and the Scales of Justice

"It is a crime that has no name."

—Winston Churchill, on realizing the
magnitude of Nazi atrocity[1]

In 1945, at the end of World War II, the Allied soldiers were sickened when they entered the German concentration camps. Winston Churchill, prime minister of England, summed up the sense of horror felt around the world with his inability to place a name on it. He also spoke accurately. No legal definition yet existed to describe the deliberate massacre of entire targeted groups of people. There was no vocabulary to describe the obliteration of

6 million Jews, 50,000 Roma (Gypsies), 50,000 homosexuals, and about 5 million others. Nations of the world had names for war crimes such as maltreatment or torture of prisoners of war, but for these crimes they had no name.

The Nuremberg Trials

Within six months of the end of the war with Germany, the first trials were held to try Nazi leaders for "crimes against humanity." The trials were conducted in Nuremberg, Germany, from November 1945 to October 1946, by the Nuremberg International Military Tribunal, which consisted of four judges, one from each of four Allied nations: the United States, Great Britain, Soviet Union, and France. Twenty-two leading Nazis stood trial. Twelve of these men were sentenced to death. Three received a sentence of life in prison, and four received long prison terms. Three were found not guilty. In addition, several Nazi organizations, including the SS, the Gestapo, and the Nazi party leadership were convicted of crimes.

Indictments specified three general types of crimes: "crimes against peace" (they planned and waged an aggressive war), "war crimes" (treatment of prisoners of war and hostages), and "crimes against humanity." That category covered crimes against civilian populations, including mass murder of racial, ethnic, or religious groups, such as the killing of European Jews.

In the words of political science scholar William

Under heavy guard, defendants at the Nuremberg Trials (1945–46) listen to the case against them.

Shawcross, "At Nuremberg . . . the real plaintiff was Civilisation itself."[2]

Many people criticized the proceedings. They were conducted by the victorious Allied nations, and some of the legal procedures used by the judges were established after the end of the war. What if the same standards had been applied to the Allies? No one was free of guilt. What about civilians killed by the dropping of atomic bombs on Hiroshima and Nagasaki in August 1945? Some critics have suggested that this act by the United States was a "crime against a civilian population." What about internment camps established for Japanese Americans in the United

States? Simply because of their ethnic origin, Japanese Americans had come under suspicion in the United States during the war, and many were imprisoned.

Nonetheless, according to Shawcross, Nuremberg stands as "one of the most important legal landmarks of the twentieth century."[3] For the first time, perpetrators were held accountable by an international tribunal for actions taken during wartime. Unlike the Armenian genocide, which had slipped by without consequence once the first cries of outrage began to wane, justice, however imperfectly, was served at Nuremberg.

Additional attention focused on the Holocaust when Adolf Eichmann stood trial in Israel. Eichmann, a Nazi official who oversaw extermination of Jews, had escaped to Argentina, where he was abducted in 1960 and delivered to Israel. There, he was tried, convicted, and hanged. The Eichmann trial, which was broadcast on television, delved deep into the details of the atrocities that had occurred in Nazi Germany. For many people worldwide, this trial came to symbolize retribution for crimes against humanity even more than the less publicly held Nuremberg trials. Nuremberg, however, set a legal precedent for international justice that would have great importance in the decades to come.

Birth of the United Nations

After World War II, a new world order was beginning to emerge. The United Nations was born just as the war against Germany and Japan came to an end. It was not the first attempt at operating a truly international organization that hoped to include all nations of the world, but it is the strongest international organization ever to emerge.

Within a year of the signing of the Charter of the United Nations and Statute of the International Court of Justice in San Francisco on June 26, 1945, the United Nations established a Commission on Human Rights. By the end of 1948, two important documents were established as the bulwark for UN activities in human rights: the Universal Declaration of Human Rights and the Convention on the Prevention and Punishment of the Crime of Genocide.

The Declaration of Human Rights

The issue of human rights was high on the agenda at the newly formed United Nations. A committee of representatives from member nations was quickly formed, headed by U.S. human rights advocate Eleanor Roosevelt. It framed a Universal Declaration of Human Rights, which was adopted by the UN General Assembly on December 10, 1948.

This landmark document established for every person on Earth equal fundamental rights with all other people, no matter where they lived, how much money they had, what ethnic background or religious beliefs they had, or what color their skin was. The idea of human rights that are more fundamental than the ruling of any government was set forward in the

American Declaration of Independence in 1776. Human rights were also set out in the Bill of Rights in the U.S. Constitution in 1789 and the French Declaration of the Rights of Man in 1791, but now the Universal Declaration of Human Rights was accepted by many nations of the world. (However, due to isolationist factions within the country during the Cold War, the United States did not ratify this document until 1986.)

Of course, the Declaration of Human Rights is not a magic wand. Saying these rights exist is not the same as being able to ensure that everyone will receive respect for his or her rights. Accomplishing that goal is the work of everyone, every day. It is also the work of the courts of justice, and the United Nations recognized that legal grounds needed to be established before any kind of international justice system could exist. The organization had already begun that process the day before passing the Declaration of Human Rights, by setting the ground-work for legal consequences for the most severe of all human rights violations: acts of genocide.

The United Nations vs. Genocide

On December 9, 1948, the UN General Assembly adopted the Convention on the Prevention and Punishment of the Crime of Genocide. Entered into force in 1951, it set forth a definition and conse-quences for the crime of genocide.

However, the United Nations is composed of so many nations having such divergent goals that compromise is at the heart of every decision. The Genocide Convention was no exception, and so the definition of genocide is, in the opinion of some, not broad enough. Some kinds of groups that have been the objects of genocide are not included. Among these are homosexuals, the mentally ill, and members of political opposition groups. These standards do not include the homosexuals who were targeted by the Nazis, or the political groups, intellectuals, or physicians who were massacred in Cambodia.

Yet some of the most outspoken advocates against genocide speak against broadening the definition, since a broader definition includes more cases, but also dilutes the meaning of the word. If "genocide" is equivalent to "mass murder," why have two terms for the same concept? If the word "Holocaust" means any extermination, then it loses the powerful identification with the Nazi extermination of 6 million Jews.

The United Nations has begun to approach this issue in another way, not by broadening the definition of genocide, but instead by bringing legal clarity to the concept of "crimes against humanity."

UN Recognition of Crimes Against Humanity

An official United Nations statement about the progress of human rights as of 1999 asserts: "The human rights abuses prevalent in internal conflicts are now among the most atrocious in the world. In 1996, there were 19 ongoing situations of internal violence around the world in which 1,000 people or more were killed. These so-called "high-intensity conflicts" cumulatively led to between 6.5 million and 8.5 million deaths. In the same year, there were also 40 "low-intensity conflicts," each causing between 100 and 1,000 deaths."[4]

In the last few years, we have come to recognize the full magnitude of these tragedies, a major step toward resolving this urgent international problem. The world's nations—including the United States— have always valued their sovereignty, the right to run their own affairs within their own borders, and to establish their own laws. These rights have always held the deepest diplomatic respect among nations. Yet many nations are beginning to recognize that, as vital as sovereignty is to national and international health, some issues are greater than these rights. The greatest of these is the violation of human rights and, specifically, the issue of genocide.

Criminal Tribunals in the 1990s

The United Nations established two criminal tribunals to deal with two specific areas in which human rights violations, war crimes, and genocide were suspected. In 1993 the International Criminal Tribunal for the former Yugoslavia (ICTY) was established in The Hague. In 1994, the International Criminal Tribunal for Rwanda (ICTR) was established in Arusha, Tanzania. For the first time, the United Nations gave the power to try war criminals to these international courts.

Indictments from The Hague have included at least nine counts of genocide. Two were leveled at Radovan Karadzic, who formerly led the Bosnian Serbs. Two also were brought against General Ratko Mladic, chief of staff of the Bosnian Serb army. In 1999, Serb president Slobodan Milosevic also was indicted by the UN prosecutor on counts of genocide, among other crimes.

The first conviction by a United Nations international tribunal was handed down by the ICTR on September 2, 1998, when Jean-Paul Akayesu, Hutu mayor of the Rwandan town of Taba, was found guilty of genocide and crimes against humanity. The tribunal based the judgment in part on testimony "that there was an intention to wipe out the Tutsi group in its entirety, since even newborn babies were not spared."[5] By the end of 1998, two more convictions followed, including that of the former prime minister of Rwanda.

Despite that, justice in Rwanda faces overwhelming challenges. More than one hundred twenty thousand Hutu people arrested on genocide charges crowded the jails in Rwanda at the end of 1998. Most of these were being tried, not by the UN's tribunal, but by Rwandan courts. Between January and November 1998, these courts tried two hundred people and sentenced about eighty of them to be executed. At that rate, as one observer points out, it would take five hundred to six hundred years to try all the defendants. As of 2000, the primarily Tutsi military continues to arrest an average of a thousand Hutu monthly on genocide charges.

Literally thousands of citizens participated in the crime, and the question remains as to how justice can be served in this small country with so much of its populace accused.[6] Nonetheless, these arrests, indictments, and convictions stand as landmarks in the case against genocide.

Justice: Its Many Forms

Yet nothing that can be done at the international level addresses the real human suffering that occurs when a nation commits genocide. Nothing can bring back the dead. We could execute all the perpetrators, and that "justice" still does nothing to comfort the orphan child or rebuild the home of a displaced refugee. Justice comes in many forms. The tribunals attempt to pay respect to the dead and the living by making the guilty pay for their crimes—though some may think the payment can never be enough. In the case of the UN tribunals, in accordance with UN regulations, no death sentences will be handed down. Trials held by individual countries, however, can and often do carry death sentences.

Never again should a leader be allowed to shrug off genocide, as Hitler did. The prospect of the consequences, including a tarnished place in history, may deter at least some would-be mass murderers.

The Politics of Justice

National governments often do not bring those who have planned and executed a genocide to justice. They fear reprisals for dark deeds committed within their own boundaries. They are reluctant to give up their national sovereignty to a greater good, an international view of justice. They fear they will lose power. They may fear that instability will result in the region, and that there will be further outbreaks of war and violence. For example, during the Nuremberg Trials, the Cold War tensions between the United States and the USSR caused the United States to pursue Nazis and fascists less relentlessly than the Russian communists wanted to do. Some political factions within the United States and other nations oppose any submission to international law, which would restrict the nation's ability to govern itself freely.

All these political pressures influence a nation's votes, for example, in the UN General Assembly (composed of all member nations, numbering 188 by 1999) and Security Council (a fifteen-member body entrusted with peacekeeping and security decisions, which are binding to all member nations). They also affect a government's willingness to participate in peacekeeping missions and other UN actions.

Within the United Nations, the structure of the Security Council favors the five permanent members: the United States, Russia, Great Britain, China, and France. The Council cannot make an effective decision if it is vetoed by any of these five permanent members. So this structure creates a special protection from prosecution for the actions of these nations.

However, in addition to the United Nations, many independent organizations now cross national boundaries and have no allegiance to individual countries, including Doctors Without Borders, Human Rights Watch, Amnesty International, and the International Medical Corps. The presence and actions of these organizations help place pressure, even though political considerations may hold back the United Nations or other international organizations, such as NATO.

A Permanent International Tribunal

People now live in a global community. Telecommunications, jet travel, and mass media shape the world. Nations' economic lives are intertwined. As the twenty-first century begins, many people see an increasing need for an equitable form of international law, backed by an international court with clear and appropriate powers. The current specific tribunals are hampered by the lack of an international police force. They can indict, but many of the indicted are still at large, and the court has no way to bring them to trial.

The UN Diplomatic Conference of Plenipotentiaries established the International Criminal Court, with its seat at The Hague, on July 17, 1998. Its power and effectiveness are still uncertain, but UN Secretary-General Kofi Annan said in a statement about the conference,

> There can be no global justice unless the worst of crimes—crimes against humanity—are subject to the law. In this age more than ever we recognize that the crime of genocide against one people truly is an assault on us all—a crime against humanity.

The establishment of an International Criminal Court will ensure that humanity's response will be swift and will be just.[7]

According to Annan's definition of the court's purpose, "Its aim is to put an end to the global culture of impunity—the culture in which it has been easier to bring someone to justice for killing one person than for killing 100,000."[8]

As Alain Destexhe puts it: "Genocide must be reinstated as the most infamous of crimes, the memory of the victims preserved and those responsible identified and brought to justice by the international community."[9]

We can only hope that we are finally traveling a path that will take us to this kind of justice.

9

What Can We Do?

"Most events of genocide are marked by massive indifference, silence, and inactivity."
—Israel W. Charny, sociologist[1]

Once begun, genocide is like a tidal wave that destroys everything and everyone in its path. The massacre of hundreds, thousands, even millions of people is more gruesome, more horrible than most of us can even imagine. What can be done to stop this wave?

Many experts in this field have given this question much careful consideration. Leo Kuper offers four major strategies: an early warning system, use of the media,

101

involvement by religious and human rights leaders, and public campaigns.[2]

On an individual level, other strategies might include: development of skills for resolving conflict positively, learning not to hate, encouraging respect for human rights, asking questions about what you see, thinking critically, looking for patterns and signs, and helping to fight crimes against humanity.

Early Warning System

The early warning signs should show that grave trouble is brewing. A group is targeted and isolated. Civil rights are limited. An atmosphere of hatred builds up. The group's property is destroyed. Members of the group suffer attacks. Derogatory slogans and names become commonplace. The government encourages animosity. Arrests are made. People disappear. Groups of militia and paramilitary troops are trained. Mass graves may be dug in advance. All these are clear and present warning signs that terrible disasters are about to begin.

The Media as Watchdog

The media's ability to get information not available to other people and to publish in print, sound and video make the media a powerful tool for justice. Journalists must have the freedom to print what they know, and they must have the responsibility to watch for the beginning signs of crimes against humanity. Photographs and stories keep people linked across national boundaries, and what is known is not easily hidden or denied. Every genocide discussed in this book was made possible through secrecy. Speaking of the power of the communications media, UN Secretary-General Kofi Annan once said, "With the help of television, we can shine a light into ever more pockets of intolerance; there is nothing those dark recesses fear more than light."[3] The media can help prevent genocide by making it public.

The media has a further responsibility, though, and an important one. It must remain independent and objective. It must never allow its use to promote bias or propaganda. Otherwise, this power tool can become an agent for genocide, as it was in Nazi Germany and Rwanda.

Religious and Human Rights Leaders Speak Out

Hitler's power stemmed from the propaganda his government promoted and religious leaders supported, his own passion and public charisma, and his ability to work the psychology of the people he led. Powerful and charismatic leaders on the side of human rights must constantly counterbalance the influence for evil that others may have. When a society becomes soaked in hatred, violence, and aggression, the voices of tolerance, peace, and humanity must be raised with equal strength.

Public Campaigns

Public campaigns for tolerance, justice, and awareness have made hiding atrocity more difficult in today's world. The establishment of memorials and museums helps heighten public awareness of past atrocities and encourages visitors to reflect upon the moral and spiritual questions raised by events such as the Holocaust. These memorials also help focus our understanding of our own responsibilities as citizens in a democracy.

What Can One Person Do?

Every national action has its roots in the beliefs and will of its citizens. Even dictators need to gain approval from the people they govern—that is why Hitler placed such a high value on the work of his minister of propaganda, Joseph Goebbels. In a democracy, the will of the government should reflect the will of the people, and the will of the people begins with each individual.

In the words of psychologist Israel W. Charny, "it is urgently necessary to make individuals far more aware than they have been of their responsibility to guard against the intrusion of attitudes that promote genocide."[4]

No intelligent person imagines that if we just all smiled at one another the world would be peaceful. Conflicts of interest exist—among people, among groups, and among nations. The key lies in knowing how to resolve conflicts constructively and positively. And in developing a set of values that promote the ability to look at things from another person's viewpoint.

The office of the UN High Commissioner for

Refugees has put together a list of skills that are useful for developing constructive, active, and nonviolent methods for resolving conflicts.[5] These include critical thinking, cooperation, appropriate assertiveness, advocacy, conflict resolution, and social literacy. Genocide and other forms of violence take hold in societies where these skills are not widely at work. If each person and small groups of people cultivate them, these skills can help lead to a more productive, positive, and peaceful world—a world in which people no longer commit genocide.

Thinking Critically

Critical thinking can be a major asset—approaching issues with both an open and critical mind, looking at the facts, and learning how to evaluate how solid these facts are. If the facts lead to a change of opinion, a critical thinker is not afraid to make an adjustment in the light of new evidence and rational arguments.

People need to be aware of other people's motives, and to look beyond the face-value appearance of statements and events. Thinking critically also means being on the alert for bias and indoctrination in oneself and in others, being ready to challenge uncritical thinking, wherever it is found, and watching out for the twisted truth of propaganda—the genocide perpetrator's favorite tool.

Building Cooperation

Some things can be accomplished best by working together toward a common goal. Give-and-take teamwork does not mean a loss of individuality, but that a person can work either alone or with others. Knowing how to get people to work together toward a positive end is a valuable asset, and effective cooperation builds bonds of mutual respect and trust.

Being Appropriately Assertive

Being assertive begins with knowing how to communicate clearly and fairly. The idea is to be assertive with others, without being either aggressive or passive, preserving respect both for their rights and one's own. Many people swing too far one way or the other. Appropriate assertiveness calls for balance and thoughtfulness, and it is one of the best methods for negotiating fair and positive resolutions to conflict.

Practicing Advocacy

When anyone's rights get trampled on, everyone loses. (Today they may come for your neighbor; tomorrow they may come for you.) The practice of advocacy means using one's assertiveness skills to speak up effectively and appropriately for others' rights, as well as one's own.

Resolving Conflict

When conflicts arise, the ability to analyze them objectively and systematically can help lead to resolution. Many conflicts arise out of misunderstandings. Often people get trapped in a position and cannot get out without losing face. When someone in the group knows how to untangle misunderstandings and suggest several solutions, or even put one or more into effect, the problem is much more likely to get resolved to everyone's satisfaction.

Achieving Social Literacy

The UN High Commissioner for Refugees calls social literacy "the ability to influence decision-making thoughtfully and constructively" toward building peace, both within one's own life and the local community, and ultimately at the national and international levels.

Defeating Genocide With Attitude

Attitudes and values such as empathy, self-respect, respect for others, global concern, environmental concern, open-mindedness, vision, and social responsibility also contribute to a world view that can "guard against attitudes that promote genocide."[6] Going even further, one person can make a difference by taking positive steps to reject hatred of the Other, promoting respect for human rights, and understanding the reality of one's own prejudices.

Refusal to Learn Hatred

Genocide builds on the back of hatred and prejudice. Prejudice includes prejudging someone because of a group that person belongs to and not on the person's actions. Prejudice and hatred are not the only ingredients that make genocide possible. However, unscrupulous leaders have used hatred and prejudice over and over to gain approval for acts of genocide.

They even have incited ordinary citizens to help them commit genocide.

What can be done on a personal level to reduce hatred in oneself and in others?

Finding out more about prominent people who belong to minority groups can help. A group of psychologists have found evidence that unconscious prejudice toward African Americans and the elderly, for example, can be decreased when people see images of people from these groups who are recognized for achievement and admired.[7]

Getting to know people from varied backgrounds also helps. The greatest fear comes from the unknown. Lieutenant Heinz Buchman was one of the few members of Battalion 101 of the Order Police who refused when ordered to kill Jewish children, women and elderly in Józefów, Poland. When asked why later, he explained, "Through my business experience, especially because it extended abroad, I had gained a better overview of things. Moreover, through my earlier business activities I already knew many Jews."[8]

Respect for Human Rights

Everyone loses when anyone's human rights are not honored. Psychologists have found that a tit-for-tat, equal-sided approach to difficult relationships results in people taking advantage of one another less frequently and treating one another with mutual respect. This also goes for rights. Respect a neighbor's rights, and the neighbor will usually return the favor.

Knowing Oneself

Everyone has prejudices, but most of us do not realize that we prejudge certain people. Or we may imagine our prejudices are "natural" because so many people around us share them that they seem like the normal way of thinking. Everyone needs to know how easy it is to fool oneself—and how easily one's perception can be colored.

One group of psychologists from the University of Washington and Yale University recognized that preferences and beliefs are often unconscious. They devised a means of getting past the difference between what we think we know about ourselves and the deep-seated attitudes that govern our decisions. They devised a test, an Implicit Association Test, which helps a person become aware of the differences between thoughts and feelings.

The Study of Genocide: Looking for Patterns and Process

No one discipline can provide the answers and insights we need for preventing future genocide. Psychology alone does not have the answers. Nor does sociology, history, religion, philosophy, ethics, politics, or government. We need interdisciplinary cooperation to explore the dynamics that sustain the process. We need to discover the patterns and processes that take

The entrance to this exhibit at the Simon Wiesenthal Center Museum of Tolerance makes a point: We are all prejudiced.

place when a whole society devotes itself to the mass annihilation of a target people or peoples.

Help Organize Against Atrocity

Many organizations are working worldwide on the problems of human rights violations, crimes against humanity, and genocide. Most of them could use help in many ways. Interested people can write to these organizations or, in many cases, contact them by e-mail. (See "Organizations to Contact.")

Never Again!

More than fifty-five years after the end of the Holocaust, remnants of the hatred and self-righteousness that allowed it to happen have still not died away. On June 18, 1999, white supremacist arsonists set off firebombs at three Jewish synagogues in the quiet town of Sacramento, the capital city of California. It was a long way from Nazi Germany, and this time, in this place, government authorities spoke out against the terrorists and rallied to the support of the synagogue members who were targeted. The FBI began an intense investigation and within weeks found and arrested suspects. Both Jewish and non-Jewish neighbors contributed to funds for rebuilding. Still, the three blazes in the early dawn echoed Kristallnacht.

A month later, a twenty-one-year-old man in Illinois shot and killed an African-American basketball coach as he walked with his children on the Friday evening before July 4 and killed an Asian man in front of his church on Independence Day. He also shot at and wounded numerous other victims over the long weekend, all of them African American, Asian, or Jewish. Attracted to hate groups, he had contributed to hate newsletters and distributed hate literature in suburban neighborhoods around his home. Yet almost no one was prepared for the rampage he set out on against minorities on the July 4 weekend.

A Jewish community center in Los Angeles became the scene of bloodshed in Los Angeles in August 1999. There, three small children, a sixteen-year-old girl, and a middle-aged woman were shot in the summer afternoon by a man with an assault rifle who entered the lobby and sprayed the area with bullets.

These events are harsh reminders that hatred can lurk in human hearts and minds and that watchfulness must always continue. "Never again!" must become more than a slogan. It must become a promise we can keep.

Chapter Notes

Chapter 1. Genocide: The Slaying of a People

1. Eric Markusen, "Genocide, Total War, and Nuclear Omnicide," *Genocide: A Critical Bibliographic Review*, ed. Israel W. Charny (New York: Facts On File, 1991), p. 229.

2. Mikhail Alekseev, quoted in translation by Robert Conquest, *The Harvest of Sorrow: Soviet Collectivization and the Terror-Famine* (New York: Oxford University Press, 1986), p. 9.

3. "Revelations from the Russian Archives: Ukrainian Famine," The Soviet Archives Exhibit, Library of Congress, January 4, 1996 <http://lcweb.loc.gov/exhibits/archives/ukra.html> (April 10, 1999).

4. Michael Dobkowski, "Appendix: Chronology of Genocide," Michael N. Dobkowski and Isidor Wallimann, *Genocide in Our Time: An Annotated Bibliography with Analytical Introductions* (Ann Arbor, Mich.: Pierian Press, 1992), p. 167.

5. Samuel Totten, "The Scourge of Genocide: Issues Facing Humanity Today and Tomorrow," *Social Education* (March 1999), p. 116.

6. Roger W. Smith, Foreword, *Caravans to Oblivion: The Armenian Genocide, 1915*, by G. S. Graber (New York: John Wiley & Sons, 1996), p. ix.

7. Samuel Totten, "Teaching about Genocide," *Social Science Record 24* (Fall 1987), cited by Graber, p. 175.

8. UN General Assembly, "The Convention on the Prevention and Punishment of the Crime of Genocide," Article 2, adopted by the General Assembly on 9 December 1948, entry into force 12 January 1951, 1997, <http://www.unhchr.ch/html/menu3/b/p_ genoci. htm> (November 9, 1999).

9. Conversation with the authors at a meeting of the Sacramento Organization for Rational Thinking, Carmichael, California, May 26, 1999.

Chapter 2. The Holocaust: Massacre of Millions

1. Daniel Jonah Goldhagen, *Hitler's Willing Executioners: Ordinary Germans and the Holocaust* (New York: Alfred A. Knopf, 1996), p. 64.

2. Ibid., p. 67.

3. Ibid., p. 173.

4. Quoted from *Trials of the Major War Criminals before the International Military Tribunal*, 38:86-94 (221-L: Hitler conference of July 16, 1941, with four of his leaders, Goering, Lammers, Rosenberg, and Keitel), by Christopher R. Browning, *Ordinary Men: Reserve Police Battalion 101 and the Final Solution in Poland* (New York: HarperCollins, 1998), p. 10.

5. Quoted by Yale F. Edeiken in "An Introduction to the Einsatzgruppen," *The Holocaust History Project, 1998–1999*, <http://www.holocaust-history.org/intro-einsatz/#xv> (December 7, 1999).

6. Ibid, p. 50.

7. Browning, p. 2.

8. Ibid., p. 72.

9. Luciana Nissim, describing her arrival in Auschwitz in "Memories of the House of the Dead," quoted by Myriam Anissimov in *Primo Levi: Tragedy of an Optimist* (Woodstock, N.Y.: Overlook Press, 1997), p. 103.

10. Cited from Primo Levi and De Benedetti, in *Minerva Medica*, by Myriam Anissimov, *Primo Levi: Tragedy of an Optimist*, translated by Steve Cox (New York: The Overlook Press, 1999), p. 111.

11. Anissimov, p. 11.

12. Anissimov, pp. 1–12; 402–406.

13. Based on Jill Rutter, *"Refugees: We Left Because We Had To"* (London, Refugee Council, 1996), pp. 66–73, cited by the United Nations High Commissioner for Refugees resources for teaching the history of genocide, n.d., <http://www.unhcr.ch/teach/tchhist/12-14jr4.htm> (December 14, 1999).

Chapter 3. The Holocaust: Why?

1. International Nuremberg trial translation, March 9, 1999, <http://www.nizkor.org/hweb/people/h/himmler-heinrich/posen/oct-04-43/ausrottung-transl-nizkor.html> (c) 1999 (December 8, 1999).

2. Leo Kuper, *Genocide: Its Political Use in the 20th Century* (New Haven, Conn.: Yale University Press, 1981), p. 4.

3. Roger W. Smith, Foreword, *Caravans to Oblivion: The Armenian Genocide, 1915*, by G. S. Graber (New York: John Wiley & Sons, 1996), p. ix.

Chapter 4. Armenian Genocide: The Denial of Mass Murder

1. Adolf Hitler in an address to his generals, just prior to invading Poland in 1939, quoted by G. S. Graber, *Caravans to Oblivion: The Armenian Genocide, 1915* (New York: John Wiley and Sons, 1996), p. 128.

2. Henry Morgenthau, U.S. Ambassador to the Ottoman Empire, quoted by Roger W. Smith in the Foreword to Graber, p. xii.

3. Richard G. Hovannisian, "The Armenian Genocide and Patterns of Denial," *The Armenian Genocide in Perspective* (New Brunswick, N.J.: Transaction Publishers, 1986), p. 130.

4. Pronouncement by the Turkish government as quoted by Hovannisian, p. 116.

5. Hovannisian, p. 114.

6. Hy Ruchlis, with Sandra Oddo, *Clear Thinking: A Practical Introduction* (Buffalo, N.Y.: Prometheus Books, 1990), p. 24.

7. Leo Kuper, "The Turkish Genocide of Armenians, 1915–1917," in Hovannisian, pp. 43–59.

8. Michael J. Arlen, *Passage to Ararat* (New York: Farrar, Straus & Giroux, 1975), pp. 278–279.

Chapter 5. Cambodia: A People Turned on Itself

1. Lindsay Murdoch, "The Dead Will Know No Peace," *The Age: Melbourne Online*, January 5, 1998, <http://www.theage.com.au/daily/980105/news/news14.html> (November 14, 1999).

2. Thida B. Mam, "Samey Pol Pot: The Pol Pot Era," 1997, <http://members.aol.com/cambodia/same.htm> (November 25, 1999). Originally published in "Called by Angka," a publication of the International Network on Holocaust and Genocide.

3. Ibid.

4. David P. Chandler, *Brother Number One: A Political Biography of Pol Pot*, rev. ed. (Boulder, Colo.: Westview Press, 1999), p. 3.

5. Gwen Knapp, "Parents Ran for Their Lives, Now Their Kids Run for Fun," *San Francisco Examiner*, May 30, 1999, p. A1.

Chapter 6. Rwanda: Incited Massacre

1. Philip Gourevitch, *We Wish to Inform You That Tomorrow We Will Be Killed with Our Families: Stories from Rwanda* (New York: Farrar, Straus & Giroux, 1998), p. 59.

2. John Stremlau, "People in Peril: Human Rights, Humanitarian Action, and Preventing Deadly Conflict," *Journal of Humanitarian Assistance*, May 1998, p. 32.

3. Boutros Boutros-Ghali, secretary-general of the United Nations 1992–1996, address to the United Nations Association of China in Beijing, 26 March 1996, United Nations Press Release SG/SM/5938.

4. Charles W. Corey, "Clinton Addresses Rwanda Genocide Survivors," United States Information Service (USIS) Washington File, Kigali, Rwanda, March 25, 1998.

Chapter 7. Bosnia and Kosovo: Genocide and "Ethnic Cleansing"

1. Elizabeth Neuffler, "Srebenica Questions Hang over Bosnia Talks," *Boston Globe*, November 15, 1995, n.p., <http://www.cco.caltech.edu/~bosnia/update/srebrenica11_3.html> (November 30, 1999).

2. "45 Dead in Kosovo Killing," *San Francisco Sunday Examiner and Chronicle*, January 17, 1999, pp. A1, A11.

3. Ibid., p. A11.

4. Application Instituting Proceedings Filed in the Registry of the Court on 20 March 1993 . . . (Bosnia and Herzegovina v. Yugoslavia (Serbia and Montenegro), n.d., <http://www.icj-cij.org/icj/idocket/ibhy/ibhyorders/ibhy_iapplication_19930320.htm> (December 15, 1999).

5. Interview with Amnesty International, April 1996, July 1996, <http://www.amnesty.org/ailib/aipub/1996/EUR/46301596.htm> (November 30, 1999).

6. David Rohde, *The Christian Science Monitor*, October 2, 1995, July 1996, <http://www.amnesty.org/ailib/aipub/1996/EUR/46301596.htm> (November 30, 1999).

7. Ibid.

8. David Wightwick, program coordinator for the International Medical Corps, in a press release from the International Medical Corps quoted at IMC site, "Notes from the Field," March 29, 1999, <http://www.imc-la.com.htm> (July 25, 1999).

9. "One Family's Story: Broken Up by War," *The Cincinnati Enquirer*, February 8, 1996, <http://enquirer.com/bosnia/stories/bosnia0208.html> (November 30, 1999).

Chapter 8. Genocide and the Scales of Justice

1. Alain Destexhe, *Rwanda and Genocide in the Twentieth Century* (New York: New York University Press, 1995), p. 2.

2. William Shawcross, "Foreword," in Destexhe, p. x.

3. Ibid.

4. "Human Rights and Conflicts," November 27, 1998, <http://www.un.org/rights/HRToday> (November 15, 1999).

5. Summary of the Judgment in Jean-Paul Akayesu Case, ICTR-96-4-T Delivered on September 2, 1998, point 17, from International Criminal Tribunal for Rwanda Web site, September 2, 1998, <http://www.un.org/ictr/english/singledocs/jpa_summary.html> (December 7,1999).

6. James C. McKinley, Jr., "Massacre Trials in Rwanda Have Courts on Overload," *The New York Times*, November 2, 1998, p. 3, quoted by Samuel Totten, "The Scourge of Genocide: Issues Facing Humanity Today and Tomorrow," *Social Education*, March 1999, p. 117.

7. Kofi Annan, "Address to the International Bar Association," New York, June 11, 1997, Press Release SG/SM/6257, containing full text, June 12, 1997, <http://www.un.org/Docs/SG/Report98/ch5.htm#icc> (accessed December 7, 1999).

8. Kofi Annan, "Report of the Secretary-General on the Work of the Organization—1998," original: English, August 27,1998, <http://www.un.org/Docs/SG/Report98/ch5.htm#icc> (December 7, 1999).

9. Destexhe, p. 15.

Chapter 9. What Can We Do?

1. Israel W. Charny, *How Can We Commit the Unthinkable? Genocide, the Human Cancer* (Boulder, Colo.: Westview Press, 1982), p. 284, cited by Erik Markusen in "Genocide, Total War, and Nuclear Omnicide," in Israel W. Charny, *Genocide: A Critical Bibliographic Review*, vol. 2 (New York: Facts on File, 1991), p. 231.

2. Leo Kuper, *The Prevention of Genocide* (New Haven, Conn.: Yale University Press, 1985), described by Israel W. Charny in "The Study of Genocide," *Genocide: A Critical Bibliographic Review*, vol. 1 (New York: Facts On File, 1988), p. 15.

3. Kofi Annan, "Address to the Second United Nations World TV Forum," New York, November 19, 1997, cited in United Nations Press Release SG/SM/6401 PI/1042

19 November 1997, p. 3, <http://www.un.org/Docs/ SG/sgsm.htm> (December 7,1999).

4. Israel W. Charny, "Early Warning, Intervention, and Prevention of Genocide," in Michael N. Dobkowski and Isidor Wallimann, *Genocide in Our Time: An Annotated Bibliography with Analytical Introductions* (Ann Arbor, Mich.: Pierian Press, 1992), p. 147.

5. Office of the UN High Commissioner for Refugees, "For Teachers: Objectives," 1999, <http://www.unhcr. ch/teach/aims.htm> (November 15, 1999).

6. Ibid.

7. In a paper presented at the June 1999 meeting of the American Psychological Society in Denver by psychologist Nilanjana Dasgupta of the University of Washington, reported by the University of Washington newsroom, June 1, 1999, <http://www.washington.edu/newsroom/ news/1999archive/06-99archive/k060199c.html> (December 7, 1999).

8. Christopher R. Browning, *Ordinary Men: Reserve Police Battalion 101 and the Final Solution in Poland* (New York: HarperCollins, 1998), p. 76.

Glossary

advocacy—Standing up for the rights of someone else whose rights are endangered.

anti-Semitism—Prejudice or hostility toward Jews (adj.: anti-Semitic).

Babi Yar—A ravine near Kiev, Ukraine, where thousands of Jews were massacred.

concentration camp—Prison camp established by the Nazis to imprison Jews and other "undesirables." Some were labor camps, where inmates were literally worked to death. Others were extermination sites, where prisoners were systematically stripped and gassed in large groups.

Einsatzgruppen—Special militia units formed by Heinrich Himmler, Hitler's chief of police, to follow behind the advancing German army and exterminate Jews and other "undesirables."

ethnic Albanian—A citizen of Kosovo whose ethnic background is Albanian; also called Kosovar Albanian.

ethnic cleansing—The removal of people of unwanted background from a territory, usually by any means—including forced march, torment, rape, and murder.

genocide—The systematic killing of a people.

ghetto—A separate, sometimes walled, area in a city or town, where a minority group is forced to live.

human rights—Natural rights that every human being is born with that transcend the laws enacted by any government.

Interahamwe—Radical Rwanda militia, composed mostly of Hutu.

Khmer Rouge—Initially, the armed wing of the Communist Party of Kampuchea (Cambodia), it became a radical communist rebel group that overtook Cambodia in 1975.

massacre—Mass killing, usually of defenseless human beings.

Nuremberg trials—Trials held after World War II, November 1945 to October 1946, of the twenty-two chief Nazi war criminals and others by an international military tribunal.

perpetrator—Someone who performs an evil or criminal act.

pillage—To rob and lay waste to property.

prejudice—An opinion based on stereotypes, without thought, knowledge, experience, and reason.

rationalization—The process of excusing one's actions based on reasonable-sounding explanations, usually thought up later.

resettlement—Return to a vacated land to take up life there again.

stereotype—An oversimplified, often inaccurate view of a group of people; a stereotype does not take complexities and individual differences into account.

Further Reading

Auschwitz: A History in Photographs. Compiled by Teresa Swiebocka. Bloomington: Indiana University Press, 1993.

Bachrach, Susan D. *Tell Them We Remember: The Story of the Holocaust*. Madison, Wisc.: Demeo Media, 1994.

Bitton-Jackson, Livia. *I Have Lived a Thousand Years: Growing Up in the Holocaust*. New York: Simon & Schuster Books for Young Readers, 1999.

Flint, David. *Bosnia: Can There Ever Be Peace?* Austin, Texas: Raintree Steck-Vaughn, 1995.

Frank, Anne. *The Diary of a Young Girl: The Definitive Edition*. New York: Doubleday, 1995.

Greenberg, Keith. *Rwanda: Fierce Clashes in Central Africa*. Woodbridge, Conn.: Blackbirch Press, 1996.

Perl, Lila, et al. *Four Perfect Pebbles: A Holocaust Story*. Fairfield, N.J.: Greenwillow Books, 1996.

Twagilimana, Aimable. *Hutu & Tutsi*. New York: Rosen Publishing Group, 1998.

West, Rebecca. *Black Lamb & Grey Falcon: A Journey Through Yugoslavia*. New York: Viking Penguin, 1995.

Organizations to Contact

Amnesty International

Amnesty International (AI) is a worldwide organization that campaigns for human rights as outlined in the Universal Declaration of Human Rights adopted by the UN General Assembly in 1948. Members can contribute to the work of the organization in many ways. AI also has an office in Washington, D.C., as well as offices in most countries of the world.

322 8th Avenue, New York, NY 10001
Phone: (212) 807-8400 / Fax: (212) 627-1451
Internet Address: <http://www.amnesty.org>
E-mail: admin-us@aiusa.org

Human Rights Watch

Human Rights Watch is dedicated to protecting the human rights of people around the world. The group acts on the behalf of victims and activists to prevent discrimination, support political freedom, protect people from war crimes, and to bring offenders to justice. The organization also has offices in Seattle; Washington, D.C.; Los Angeles; London; and Brussels. (See "Internet Addresses" for more information.)

350 Fifth Avenue, 34th Floor,
New York, NY 10118-3299
Phone: (212) 290-4700 / Fax: (212) 736-1300
E-mail: rwnyc@hrw.org

Simon Wiesenthal Center Museum of Tolerance

The Simon Wiesenthal Center was established to memorialize the Holocaust and it victims. It also tries to promote awareness of the damage caused by hate and prejudice.

9786 West Pico Boulevard, Los Angeles, CA 90035
Phone: (310) 553-9036 / Fax: (310) 553-8007
E-mail: webmaster@wiesenthal.com

United States Holocaust Memorial Museum

Education Department: education@ushmm.org. Use this address for all inquiries for educational materials and for inquiries by students seeking materials for school projects. (For other e-mail addresses and phone numbers at the museum, see "Internet Addresses.")

100 Raoul Wallenberg Place, SW
Washington, D.C. 20024-2150
Phone: (202) 488-0400

Internet Addresses

Amnesty International

<http://www.amnesty.org>

Describes the activities of Amnesty International, a worldwide organization that campaigns for human rights as outlined in the Universal Declaration of Human Rights adopted by the UN General Assembly in 1948.

Frontline: The Triumph of Evil

<http://www.pbs.org/wgbh/pages/frontline/shows/evil>

A report on the Rwanda genocide and how the United Nations and the West ignored warnings of the 1994 Rwanda genocide and turned its back on the victims of the genocide.

Human Rights Watch

<http://www.hrw.org>

This online site provides up-to-date, detailed reports of the Human Rights Watch's investigations into violations of human rights worldwide. (See "Organizations to Contact.")

Implicit Association Test

<http://buster.cs.yale.edu/implicit/>

This site offers a psychological test that helps compare the difference between thoughts and feelings about other people—between what you think your attitude is and what your real feelings are. Try it.

Places to Visit

Simon Wiesenthal Center Museum of Tolerance

The Simon Wiesenthal Center presents special events related to tolerance and the Holocaust. It has an extensive educational program called "Teaching the Steps of Tolerance." In addition, the Center's Museum of Tolerance attracts thousands of visitors. Interactive exhibits encourage reflection by exploring personal prejudice, the effects of hate, the existence of hate groups in the United States, and similar themes. The Hall of Testimony shows remarkable accounts of heroism and sacrifice by those who lived during the Holocaust.

9786 West Pico Boulevard, Los Angeles, CA 90035
Phone: (310) 553-9036 / Fax: (310) 553-8007

United States Holocaust Memorial Museum

The U.S. Holocaust Memorial Museum maintains a permanent exhibition in memory of the victims of the Holocaust, in addition to shorter-term exhibits on aspects of Jewish life in Europe, the Holocaust, and related events. The museum was chartered by a unanimous act of Congress in 1980.

100 Raoul Wallenberg Place, SW
Washington, D.C. 20024-2150
<http://www.ushmm.org/>
Phone: (202) 488-2606
E-mail: group_visit@ushmm.org

Index

A

Albania, 13, 86
Albanians, ethnic, in Kosovo, 77, 85–86
Allies (World War I), 23, 28
Allies (World War II), 31, 38, 88, 90
American Indian, 11–12
Amnesty International, 99
Annan, Kofi, 99–100, 103
anti-Semitism, 20-23, 27, 40
Argentina, 13, 91
Arlen, Michael J., 52
Armenia, 16, 36, 39, 44, 45–53, 73, 82, 91
Austria, 27
Auschwitz, 33–35

B

Babi Yar, 5–6, 29
Balkan region, 17, 64, 75, 76–78, 86
Bangladesh, 13
Barbarossa decree, 28
Battalion 101, 31–32, 41, 108
Bill of Rights, U.S., 93
Birkenau, 25
Bosnia, 13, 70, 76–87
Boutros-Ghali, Boutros, 70
Britain, 23, 28, 49, 89, 98
Browning, Christopher R., 31–32
Buchenwald, 25, 34
Burundi, 13, 65, 68, 71

C

Cambodia, 13, 16, 37, 42, 54–64, 72, 73, 94
Charny, Israel W., 101, 104

China, 8, 55, 56, 98
Churchill, Winston, 88
Clinton, President Bill, 73
Cold War, 93, 98
concentration camps, 25-26, 88
crimes against humanity, 80, 89, 91, 74, 76, 99, 102, 110
Croatia, 17, 78
Czechoslovakia, 27

D

Dachau, 25,26
Death camps, 32–36
Declaration of Independence, U.S., 93
Declaration of the Rights of Man, France, 93
Democratic Republic of Congo, 65, 74
Destexhe, Alain, 80, 100
disabled, 14
Doctors Without Borders, 99

E

East Timor, 13
Eichmann, Adolf, 91
Einsatzgruppen, 28–30, 32
El Salvador, 13
"ethnic cleansing," 16, 79-80
ethnocide, 12, 16
extermination camps, see death camps

F

Final Solution, 19, 32-35. 39, 40, 41, 52
France, 23, 28, 49, 55, 89, 98

G

genocide
 definition, 14–17, 61
 justice and, 88–100
 responsibility for, 17–18
 stages of, 36–37
 UN Convention on the
  Prevention and
  Punishment of the
  Crime of, 15, 92,
  93–94
Germany, 14, 19–37, 38–44,
 49, 62, 79, 82, 89, 91,
 103, 111
Gestapo (Geheime
 Staatspolizei), 26, 29, 89
ghetto, 20–21
Goebbels, Joseph, 26, 27,
 104

H

Hamid, Sultan Habdul, 46
Himmler, Heinrich, 29, 38
Hitler, Adolf, 6, 19, 23-30,
 34, 39, 40, 41, 43, 45
 62, 97, 103–104
Holocaust, 14, 15, 16,
 19–44, 73, 88, 91, 94,
 104, 110
homosexuals, 14, 89, 94
Human Rights
 UN Commission on, 92–93
 Universal Declaration of,
 92–93
Human Rights Watch, 99
Hutu, 66–75, 96

I

Indochina, Union of, 55
Interahamwe militia, 71, 72
International Court of Justice,
 80, 92
International Criminal Court,
 99
International Criminal
 Tribunal for Rwanda
 (ICTR), 73, 95–96
International Criminal
 Tribunal for the former

Yugoslavia (ICTY), 16,
 64, 95
International Medical Corps,
 86, 99
internment camps, 90–91

J

Japan, 55, 92
Japanese Americans, 90–91
"Jewish problem," the, 19,
 21–22
Jews, genocide against, see
 Holocaust

K

Karadzic, Radovan, 96
Khmer Empire, 55
Khmer Rouge, 56–60
Kigari V, King, 67
Kosovo, 13,64, 77, 78,
 83–87
Kristallnacht (Night of Broken
 Glass), 27, 111
Kuper, Leo, 41, 51, 101

L

Lager Nordhausen, 42
Lemkin, Raphael, 14
Levi, Primo, 35–36

M

Macedonia, 78, 86
McWhirter, Cameron, 86
mentally ill, 14, 94
Mille Collines, 70,74
Milosevic, Slobodan, 64, 85,
 96
Montenegro, 78, 86
Munich Convention of 1938,
 28
Musmanno, Justice Michael,
 30

N

Nanking, 13
National Socialist German
 Workers party, see Nazi:
 party
Nazi, 14, 19, 23–24, 26,
 38–44, 89–91, 94, 98
party, 6, 26, 89

Nissim, Luciana, 33–34
North Atlantic Treaty
    Organization (NATO), 68,
    84, 99
North Vietnam, 55, 56
Ntaryamira, Cyprien, 68
Nuremberg
    Laws, 24
    trials, 30, 48, 90, 91, 98
Nuremberg International
    Military Tribunal, 89

O

Oranienburg, 25
Order Police, 29m 30–32,
    41, 108
Ottoman Empire, 46-47, 50,
    53

P

Pale of Settlement, Russia, 21
Phnom Penh, 56–57, 60, 64
pogrom, 9, 21
Poland, 14, 28, 30–32, 35,
    105
Pol Pot, 42, 54, 56, 59, 62,
    64

R

Red Cross, International
    Committee of (ICRC), 82
Roma (Gypsies), 14, 89
Roosevelt, Eleanor, 92
Rugova, Ibrahim, 83
Russia, 21, 23, 28, 46, 48,
    49, 53, 98
Rwanda, 13, 14, 16, 65–75,
    78, 84, 96–97, 103

S

Serbia, 64, 77, 78, 83,
    84–85
Sihanouk, King Norodom, 55
Slovenia, 17, 78
Smith, Roger W., 43
Somalia, 70
South Vietnam, 55–56
Srebrenica, 81–83
SS (Schutzstaffel), 26, 29,
    38, 39, 89
Stalin, Joseph, 10

Suljic, Hurem, 82

T

Tanzania, 65, 71, 74, 95
Tito, Josip Broz, 78
Trapp, Major Wilhelm, 31–32
Treblinka, 35
Turkey, 10, 39, 44, 45–53
Tutsi, 66–75, 96
Twa, 66

U

Uganda, 71
Ukraine, 5–6, 9–10
Union of Soviet Socialist
    Republics (USSR), 11,
    17, 69
United Nations (UN), 15–16,
    64, 68, 70, 75, 91–100
Assistance Mission for
    Rwanda (UNAMIR), 68
General Assembly, 15, 92,
    93, 98
High Commissioner for
    Refugees, 104–105,
    107
Security Council, 98
United States (U.S.), 11–12,
    20, 23, 30, 56, 64, 70,
    73, 89, 90-91, 93, 95,
    98

V

Voice of the Patriot, 74

W

Waffen-SS, 29
World War I, 22, 23, 44
World War II, 6, 19, 28, 38,
    40, 41, 55, 80, 88, 91
Wounded Knee, 11–12

Y

Young Turk political party,
    47–50
Yugoslavia, former, 14, 17,
    37, 78–79, 95

Z

Zaire (now the Democratic
    Republic of Congo), 65,
    71–72